Patterns Illuminating

How Jesus Opens the Heart

A New Passage Through the Gospels

by

Damian and Christina Vraniak

First Published in 2016 by Waubishmaa'inagan/Whitewolf Press, W3177 Hamilton Road, Springbrook, Wisconsin 54875-9413 USA

The information in this book is true and complete to the best of our knowledge. All recommendations are made without any guarantee on the part of the author or Publisher, who also disclaim any liability incurred in connection with the use of this data or specific details.

Library of Congress Cataloging-in-Publication data

Vraniak, Damian A. & Christina C.
    Patterns Illuminating How Jesus Opens the Heart: A New Passage Through the Gospels
    text by Damian A. and Christina C. Vraniak
        p. cm.
    Includes bibliographic references
    ISBN-13: 978-0-9758903-8-7 (softbound)
    ISBN-10: 0-9758903-8-7 (softbound)
        1. The Teachings of Jesus. 2. Bible Study.
        I. Vraniak, Damian A. II. Title. III. Series.
        BS2415 2016

Library of Congress Control Number: 2016900702

Printed in the USA
10 9 8 7 6 5 4 3 2 1

Dedication

Our son, *Daybreak Borne Vraniak*, will be born soon and we wish to dedicate this study of the Gospels to him. May *'Little Day'* find upon his birth two parents who are one in their love for their beloved Jesus Christ and may the love of their Lord come into Daybreak as each new day dawns with the brilliant light of His Saving Grace.

Acknowledgements

We would like to offer our appreciation to Kent Seldahl, David McKee, Louise and Paul Dauphinais, for reviewing early versions of the book and offering us general comments that were very helpful in improving the clarity of our presentation of this material.

A thank you goes out to Brent and Jewels Niccum for their generous support of our endeavors in writing and publishing our previous book, *Light Musing and Brief Illuminations of the Love Between Beauty and Truth*, and for this book, as well.

(The photo of the morning glory on the front and back covers was taken by Damian. The morning glory is a vine and it opens - unfurls to full bloom - to the sun in the early morning, at daybreak. It was first known by many peoples for its medicinal properties, especially contained in its seeds. It has exceptional culinary uses and many do not know that the *sweet potato* is of the extensive morning glory family. Not unimportant to us are also the allusions to *Daybreak's* Hochunk ggreat grandmother, *Glory of the Morning.*)

Preface

When placed and organized in chronological order, the four Gospels of Matthew, Mark, Luke and John reveal the beautiful design of the method Jesus uses to teach his disciples and the world. Each lesson begins with an issue or challenge presented to Jesus, to which he gives opportunity for men and women to respond. After their response Jesus offers his response, and then makes a concrete demonstration of the principles he teaches.

The four-part structure of each lesson contains:

> The Issue or Challenge
> The Response of Men and Women
> The Response of Jesus
> The Demonstration by Jesus

Once this remarkable design is recognized, it is possible to see that there are 32 (plus 1) discrete lessons that, amazingly, cluster themselves into groups of four. An exquisite sequence is revealed whereby, over time, Jesus guides his disciples by focusing on individual reality within each one, interpersonal relationship between one another, social relations among many, and sacred restoration. After focusing upon typical obstacles to responding beneficially in these layers for his disciples, Jesus deals with the challenges that corporate community and religious institutions present for those seeking a path and portal to the spiritual kingdom of heaven.

Lessons structure themselves in cluster of four:

Lessons 1-4: *God gifts His Son*

Lessons 5-8: *Jesus directs how to receive God's Gift <u>within</u> each person*
Lessons 9-12: *Jesus teaches about relationship <u>between</u> each one and another*
Lessons 13-16: *Jesus teaches about relations <u>among</u> family, groups & communities*

Lessons 17-20: *Jesus teaches disciples how the path to heaven may be obstructed*
within, between & among
Lessons 21-24: *Jesus engages the institutions of man*
Lessons 25-28: *Jesus portrays the kingdom of heaven*
Lessons 29-32: *Jesus demonstrates the authority of the kingdom of heaven over*
the institutions of man

Lessons 33: *Jesus rises, returns and begins the Christian church through the Holy*
Spirit

Using a chronological Bible (see Zondervan's *NIV Integrated Study Bible* (2013)), this study guide offers four lessons each month to groups seeking a new way to read, explore and understand the Gospels. The suggested form for doing the study is for pairs (or couples) to study each lesson together during the week and then come together with other couples and pairs at the end of the week. The group discusses the entire cluster of four lessons on the fourth or fifth week of the month.

A new, innovative, small group process of reading Scripture and praying, involving a sequence of individual self-reflection, pair-dialogue, pair-sharing to the group, group conversation, and inter-group discussion is offered (see Appendix A). A group may use either a generic form of this unique small group process or a more spiritually informed version called *Dialectio Communitas Divina* (see page 14 and Appendix E).

And an exploration of the parables Jesus told is made by clustering these 'little stories' into groups of four interrelated stories that build progressively upon one another. One cluster of sixteen stories is configured and explored in relationship to the first sixteen lessons. A second cluster of sixteen stories is arranged and examined within the second sixteen lessons. It seems that the 4x4 design holds together quite nicely not only for the lessons, but for the little stories (parables) embedded within the lessons, as well. The stories remaining after arranging these 32 parables in concert with the 32 lessons actually compose an overall orientation to the whole study (see Appendix B):

Four by Four Pattern Also Evident in the 'Little Stories' of Jesus

> First Cluster of Four Stories: *Light for the World*
> Second Cluster of Four Stories: *In the Care of the Father*
> Third Cluster: *Come as Little Children to Me and to the Kingdom of Heaven*
> The Fourth and Final Cluster of Four Stories: *Enter the Kingdom of Heaven*

Table of Contents

FIRST FOUR CLUSTERS OF LESSONS (4x4):

SECOND FOUR CLUSTERS OF LESSONS (4X4):

Introduction

"I've sometimes puzzled at missionaries abroad who speak of needing resources, curriculums to teach by," the department head settled back in his chair, "because you have the Bible, right? Teach from that." I silenced my surprise and let our casual catch-up take its course. I had been a graduate of his department, one well liked by the religion professors, but I'd never quite heard this simple philosophy. The Bible was all I'd had when I taught in Bethlehem for a few years, ~~as~~ though I had really wanted a curriculum to tell me how to teach it.

When my husband and I began to read through the Gospels in Zondervan's Chronological Bible, I had a few low-lying ambitions. I wanted to better understand the order of events in Jesus' life and ministry. I thought maybe I'd gain a clearer understanding of who the Holy Spirit is, and what a life embodied by him looks like.

Truthfully, these ambitions were both passive aggressive and honest. I wanted to know why today's Christians, myself included, lack so much of what Jesus and His disciples had, why we don't do what they did. I thought if I knew more, I could both accuse the Church of her lack, yet somehow have the same void in me filled. So I sought to discover how to become one with humble faith that surrenders the home of my heart to the Holy Spirit; surrenders to being healed, and healing, to listening and speaking, to casting out evil, and to raising the dead – both in the physical and spiritual sense. I wanted to know from Jesus what He said followers were to be like. I wanted to know how what He'd given his followers enabled them to remain so in the lives they lived, and the deaths they died. I wanted to better understand who Jesus says the Holy Spirit is, and how the Holy Spirit lives in a life – in my life. And while these ambitions were both ignoble and noble, I was given a different gift altogether: a method.

Jesus had a method, an organization to teaching.; one not only of knowledge, but of experiential learning. He would let an issue arise, allow others their two cents worth, then provide his own teaching on the issue, and end with an applicable, real life, demonstration of His teaching that addressed the issue, and corrected others' input. Again and again, I found the method humble; and then I found emotional security in the consistency with which Jesus used this method. He was constant whether the issue was great or small. And while I valued the content of Jesus' teachings and doings, I found myself intrigued by his constant pattern. I began to ask a new set of questions: If Jesus would demonstrate his teaching in people's lives, could he also demonstrate these principles in my life? What if I dared not just to read the content Jesus taught, but dared to open my life to His experiential teaching? What if I let God order the events of my life around a principle He wanted to teach me? What if this new habit became one of experiencing, of practicing Jesus' principles, not just knowing them?

Christina Vraniak, January 2016

I am a scientist, steeped in the experimental method and published in peer-reviewed journals, a clinician versed in evidence-based inquiry and treatment, and an author of manuals and books concerning service delivery. I care about those I serve. In the course of our study of the Gospels, I found the most brilliant, cohesive and coherent manual concerning human beings and their relationships with one another that I had ever read.

I am a father and grandfather, uncle and grand uncle, experienced in understanding and caring for the development of children. And I am a husband and father. This book is written humbly out of the love for my lovely wife, Christina, and our little son soon to be born. However, my love for God the Father and Creator is imperfect. My love for God the Son and Savior is insufficient. My continuing efforts to empty and open to God the Holy Spirit continue to be inadequate. In spite of the meagerness of such efforts at love, such love is the context for this study guide.

Most importantly, I am a *child of God*, baptized and confirmed a Christian. I am descended through the original three generations of women in my family who were raised in the 1600's by the Christian mystic Marie Guyart (of the Incarnation), recently sainted by Pope Francis. My part of our study of the Gospels is especially in harmony with these traditions. Yet it is the experience of my confirmation and first communion upon which rests my heart for this little study guide shared with you:

... and as I was given the bread that is his body and the wine that is his blood, I was suffused with a surpassing surrender and opened with a penetrating, enveloping and encompassing light of love that brought joy to my heart and tears to my eyes ...

When asked what is most important, twice in the New Testament Jesus confirmed it is to 'love your God with all your heart, all your soul, all your strength [body], and all your mind'. In this simple, clear and most challenging directive I find the *sequence* a most telling feature for me personally. It is to begin with your heart, which deepens your soul, which, in turn, eventually directs your actions appropriately. It is only at the last, at the end, that the mind specifies some of the relevant and appropriate details. The danger for me is that it is so tempting to start with the mind, hoping to bring along the heart later on, that must be contradicted.

So it was when my wife introduced me to the chronological Bible, of which I had never heard, as we began to study Scripture together. It was so exciting and then touching to see the expressions of Mathew and John, Luke and Mark, laid side by side in all their confirming similarities and vibrant, life-giving differences. Early each morning I would become so deeply engaged as we proceeded along in our reading aloud, study and conversation, prayer. And, at some point in these heart-touchings, I noticed the basic pattern ... that some issue was presented to Jesus, that he allowed men and women to respond, before he invariably responded in principle and finally in demonstration.

As we continued to study the Gospels we realized that this map of the masterful method of Jesus, as described in the witnessing of the Gospel writers, unfolded in a perceptible sequence. It provided us with a different way of seeing and hearing beyond the more typical microanalysis of a single passage or phrase, or even a single story or parable. Once we knew we were in this unfolding method, we looked just at the first part of the lesson and the last part – the 'issue' and the 'demonstration'. We found that Jesus invariably answered the issue, challenge or question presented to him at the beginning of the lesson, in a demonstration at the end of the lesson in an exact way. His demonstration is always a very specific response and answer to the issue or challenge at the beginning. And, as importantly, the demonstration using physical healing and miraculous signs is always linked to an exact, specific, and more important spiritual principle, restoration and integration. The gift of this spiritual aspect of the physical manifestation of Jesus's healing demonstrations is the more significant, and the more difficult to discern.

In addition, over the course of the four demonstrations in the cluster of four lessons a thematic sequence developed and accumulated that helped us see direction for developing our understanding and skills, as well as their application. It was like, 'oh, this is a bike; this is how to get on the bike; this is how to ride the bike with training wheels on flat terrain; and this is how you know when you are a cyclist watching out for traffic, fixing a flat tire, and going on a cross country journey.' We had gotten much further along than 'these are the parts of bike' that just focusing on a single passage got us.

Now we can see, amazingly, that the first 4 clusters of 16 lessons sequence God's gift of his son and his son's gift of how to see and receive this gift within, between and among us. And the second set of four clusters of 16 lessons sequence an understanding of God's intention to make the kingdom of heaven available to us: It opens the path and portal through which we must travel to enter that kingdom. It shows us who will carry us successfully along that path and through the portal as we falter and fail in doing so. It shows us that the internal portal (our hearts) must be opened and surrendered by our choice, in order for our Lord to enter our souls, that he might do that compassionate caring and carrying (love) that saves us from ourselves.

So here you have what we have found providentially, through the Holy Spirit, in a brief guide to study the four Gospels for pairs, couples and others in small groups. We suggest that you find a chronological Bible (we used Zondervan's), read and study one lesson per week, a cluster of four lessons each month, with a consideration of all four lessons on the fourth or fifth week of the month. (We found it helpful to make a copy of the general outline of the *Table of Contents* in order to locate where we were in the pattern of clusters and sets of lessons.) You would thus finish in about eight months. Of course, you could make it more intense by doing a lesson a day and a cluster of four lessons in a week for eight weeks as we did, but sometimes busy schedules prevent such intensity.

As Christina expressed above, we need a better scaffold to still our bodies, calm our hearts, quiet our minds, empty and open ourselves to the portal that is Jesus Christ, in order that the Holy Spirit might mend and tend, teach and heal the fabric of our souls, in ways that are still available to us, and in ways that are exactly the manner in which the Holy Spirit acted for Jesus, his disciples, the Apostles and for many saints and sinners since. May this small offering bring to you some greater access to the love and peace available to you with the study of the Gospels, in the manner it has for us.

Damian Vraniak, January 2016

Small Group Study and Learning Process: *Learning in Pairs*

Let's say you have 36 members of your church who would like to use this guide to study the Gospels together. Study group participants can be broken up into three small collaborative learning groups called Bible Study Groups. Study Groups are composed of 3-5 pairs of members and two small group co-facilitators. Group members systematically shift who they are paired with every four sessions until everyone in each small collaborative learning group has been paired with every other member of that small group. Learning (study) activities sequentially rotate through **self-study & reflection, pair-dialogue, pair-sharing within small group, group discussion and consensus, and inter-group sharing**.

The process is as important as the sequence for each study session:

1) *Individual Condition Report*: Each person in the group takes only 30 seconds to express his preparation, knowledge-base and biases [5 minutes]

2) *Interpersonal Processing; Pair-Dialogue*: Each pair processes the information and finds a succinct summary statement encapsulating the most important aspects of their dialogue [10 minutes]

3) *Pair-Sharing*: One person from each pair presents their findings [5 minutes]

4) *Social Processing; Consensus-Forming*: The group discusses and reaches consensus listing (inclusion, order) of summary statements; [10 minutes]

This first round of processing takes about 30 minutes and is focused upon what each person read during the week, what they got out of it in general, and between the two of them what one important pearl or gem is that they would like to share with the other pairs in the study group. This is much like your typical Bible study where everyone seems to find something in the Word that resonates with something currently going on in their lives.

However, the second round, also taking about 30 minutes, is focused specifically upon what the issue is that is presented to Jesus and what is his final demonstration in response to the issue, problem or challenge, both in physical terms and in terms of the ever-present spiritual dimension of each demonstration. A generic session process is described in more detail on the next page, while a more deeply spiritually-informed process is detailed on the following page in the form of *Dialectio Communitas Divina*.

Participants in the three distinct study groups may be mixed over the course of the year, say every three months, so that each participant can experience pairing with members of other sub-groups, facilitating a larger church cohesion.

Generic Small Study Group Process Format

Each Session in the group process described here follows essentially the same template, beginning in the sacred (prayer), moving to *within* the individual, *between* paired 'buddies', then to discussion *among* the group, then back down through those layers to return and close back in the sacred (prayer).

○   Begin by holding hands forming a Circle, with a moment of PRAYER by the chaplain-du-jour (last person to arrive may get playfully designated with this).

1A   Within - Individual Condition Reports
Each individual around the circle gives a brief description of "what condition my condition is in" and any observations they may have on their preparations and readiness for the gathering.

1B   Within - Individual Activity : SELF-REFLECTION
This is an individual reflection about the focus of the session. Usually reflective in nature (jot notes), it provides material that is shared with the buddy next.

2   Between – With your Buddy :: PAIR-DIALOGUE
Buddy pairs move to a discreet distance in sight of the others, to have some one-to-one talk. This begins with sharing thoughts, feelings and/or sensations pertaining to the individual task. In discussing these, the goal is to be on the lookout for "gems" you may discover together in your learning about the material at hand; decide which of you will be 'mouthpiece' to voice this finding to the group. Return to the group circle.

3   Among – Sharing with the Group ::: PAIR-SHARING & GROUP DISCUSSION
Go around the circle, each mouthpiece voicing their pair's offering, with some brief additions from the partner as needed. While others speak, listen attentively, without interruption or commentary. Discussion will follow and should be aimed at "crystallizing" the group's understandings of the key concepts from the session.

2   Between – With your Buddy :: PAIR-DIALOGUE
Based on the group's discussion, talk briefly with the aim of deepening the fullness of how you represent the key concepts, and about what you will be doing for your midweek meeting together. Set a location, date and time to meet with your buddy. (Experience shows it to be best if this is a couple of days before the next meeting of the group.)

1   Within - Individual Commentary : SELF-REFLECTION
Like the "condition report", this is a time in which each person comments on whatever stands out in their heart/mind in response to the proceedings.

○   Close by returning to the Circle in PRAYER, then depart.

Dialectio Communitas Divina

1. Individual Self-reflection: As an individual, read, meditate upon, pray within, and contemplate the Scripture.   (***Instruct*** ... recognize & preserve Beauty)

This reflection is emptying oneself of a day's business, or preconceived ideas, and opening to God in the Word in order to attend to the presence of God speaking through Scripture to one's heart. See & believe. Hear & Follow.
(Psalm 46:10; Romans 10:8-10; John 14:27; 1 Corinthians 2:9-10)

One first slowly reads Scripture, which leads to meditation on the significance of the text, which in turn leads the person to respond in prayer. When prayer settles one in the quiet stillness-of the presence of God, contemplate Him. The four steps of this "ladder" of prayer (*Lectio Divina*), in Latin, are *lectio, meditatio, oratio,* and *contemplatio.*

2. Pair-Dialogue: With your partner, read, examine, make contrition/repent, pray.
                    (***Illuminate*** ... reconcile & restore Love)

One person gently refracts another person's examination of his/her relationship with the Lord, in pair dialogue. This refraction is an examination of one's life in order to attach to God's presence and instruction. Feel remorse at failure. Repent. (John 1:18; John 8:16; John 14:16; John 20: 20-23; Mark 6:7-13; Luke 10: 1-22; James 5:16)

In this partnering, we draw closer to what it was for Jesus to always be in and with God the Father, for the disciples to be sent out in pairs, for the apostles to later pair together – as in Paul of Tarsus and Ananias of Damascus, or as when Paul mentored Timothy, then Titus. In Church history this method of pair-dialogue was used when Benedict of Nursia integrated Cassian's guidelines into what is now known as the Rule of Saint Benedict for spiritual direction, accompaniment and companionship. The Russian *starets* and the Jewish *Hashpa'ah* and *mishpi'a*, as well as the Catholic *Sacraments of Penance & Reconciliation* are further examples of this partnering method.

3. Pair-sharing to group: As a group, read, share, converse, pray.

A spokesman of the pair shares with the group what the two have found, that the whole group may share, converse and pray together. This revelation is a seeking and sharing of forgiveness in community. Witness the Word into Works. Share salvation, save souls.   (***Inform*** ... reveal & conserve Truth)

The public reading of the Torah in the synagogue was part of Jewish tradition that Jesus made regular practice of (Luke 4:16-20; 16:29). During early Christianity, the letters of the Apostles circulated among the early churches to be read aloud for the Church's edification. These letters were later canonized into the New Testament (Colossians 4:16; 1 Thessalonians 5:27), and are a regular part of today's Lection.

4. Blessing and Benediction: Convey transformation.

(***Inspire*** ... sanctify & consecrate the Sacred)

Use the group discussion to grasp new truth, to be shared with your partner, and set inside yourself as a building block of faith. This re-composing is finding the comfort and peace of atonement. Be re-born and begin anew.

Prelude

John begins the New Testament with an overall summary of the Gospels and offers us the first glimpse of the four-part pattern:

John1: 1-18 In the beginning was the Word, and the Word was with God, and the Word was God. He was with God in the beginning. Through him all things were made; without him nothing was made that has been made. In him was life, and that life was the light of all mankind. The light shines in the darkness, and the darkness has not overcome it. There was a man sent from God whose name was John. He came as a witness to testify concerning that light, so that through him all might believe. He himself was not the light; he came only as a witness to the light.

[*The Issue*] The true light that gives light to everyone was coming into the world.

[*Response of the People*] He was in the world, and though the world was made through him, the world did not recognize him. He came to that which was his own, but his own did not receive him. Yet to all who did receive him, to those who believed in his name, he gave the right to become children of God— children born not of natural descent, nor of human decision or a husband's will, but born of God.

[*God's Response*] The Word became flesh and made his dwelling among us.

[*God's Demonstration*] We have seen his glory, the glory of the one and only Son, who came from the Father, full of grace and truth. (John testified concerning him. He cried out, saying, "This is the one I spoke about when I said, 'He who comes after me has surpassed me because he was before me.'") Out of his fullness we have all received grace in place of grace already given. For the law was given through Moses; grace and truth came through Jesus Christ. No one has ever seen God, but the one and only Son, who is himself God and is in closest relationship with the Father, has made him known.

Lessons 1-4

God Fulfills His Promise and Makes a New Covenant: *God Gifts His Son*

1. The Preparation: John the Baptist (Luke 1:1-25; 57-80)

a. The issue: God prepares a new relationship -   John the Baptist
b. The response to God's initiation: man/woman -   Zachariah/Elizabeth
c. God's plan & principle   -   Adam-Abraham-David-Jesus
d. God's Demonstration   -   birth of John

2. The Initiation: Jesus (Luke 1:26-80; Matthew 1:1-25, 2:1-7; Luke 2:1-12, 3:23-38)

a. The issue: God offers a new relationship   -   His Son
b. The response to God's initiation: man/woman   -   Joseph/Mary
c. God's plan & principle   -   Adam-Abraham-David-Jesus
d. God's Demonstration   -   birth of Jesus, Temple purification, Magi

3. The Maturation: The Child Jesus (Matthew 2:13-17; Luke 2:39-3:23; Mark 1:1-11; John 1:19-34)

a. The issue: God offers & protects His Child   -   Egypt/ Herod
b. The response to His Child   -   Simeon/ Anna
c. God's plan & principle   -   young Jesus in the Temple
d. God's Demonstration   -   John the Baptist; baptism of Jesus

4. The Spiritual Testing: In the Wilderness with Satan
(Mat 4:1-11 & 21:12-13; Mark 1:12-13 & 11:15-17; Luke 4:1-13 &19:45-46; John1:35-2:12)

a. The issue: Does Jesus belong to God?   -   Jesus goes to wilderness; Satan
b. The response to Jesus' presence   -   Satan offers nurture, support, power
c. Jesus response   -   worship only God
d. God's Demonstration   -   Satan leaves and angels attend Jesus
d. Jesus' demonstration   -   call disciples (man), water to wine (woman), clears the Temple

<u>Lesson 1.</u> *Preparation: God prepares for the coming of his son with John the Baptist*

ISSUE. *Luke 1: 13-18* But the angel said to him: "Do not be afraid, Zechariah; your prayer has been heard. Your wife Elizabeth will bear you a son, and you are to call him John. He will be a joy and delight to you, and many will rejoice because of his birth, for he will be great in the sight of the Lord. He is never to take wine or other fermented drink, and he will be filled with the Holy Spirit even before he is born. He will bring back many of the people of Israel to the Lord their God. And he will go on before the Lord, in the spirit and power of Elijah, to turn the hearts of the parents to their children and the disobedient to the wisdom of the righteous—to make ready a people prepared for the Lord." Zechariah asked the angel, "How can I be sure of this? I am an old man and my wife is well along in years."

DEMONSTRATION. *Luke 1: 57-66* When it was time for Elizabeth to have her baby, she gave birth to a son. Her neighbors and relatives heard that the Lord had shown her great mercy, and they shared her joy. On the eighth day they came to circumcise the child, and they were going to name him after his father Zechariah, but his mother spoke up and said, "No! He is to be called John." They said to her, "There is no one among your relatives who has that name." Then they made signs to his father, to find out what he would like to name the child. He asked for a writing tablet, and to everyone's astonishment he wrote, "His name is John." Immediately his mouth was opened and his tongue set free, and he began to speak, praising God. All the neighbors were filled with awe, and throughout the hill country of Judea people were talking about all these things. Everyone who heard this wondered about it, asking, "What then is this child going to be?" For the Lord's hand was with him.

Our Reflection: *Can I believe what I see and what I hear, however amazing, shocking and unlikely?* First Zachariah's fear and then his focus upon his and his wife's condition – their advanced age – flooded his heart and filled his mind so that the incoming of God's word, delivered by the angel Gabriel, is obstructed, prevented - disbelieved, disputed. So that nothing more comes out of Zachariah, he is silenced, until after 10 months of the indwelling of God's word and gift has rendered Zachariah humble, the first words written upon the coming true of God's word is what he was told by Gabriel, "His name is John," and the first words outflowing from his lips were then praise for God, as it had been demonstrated that God's word was true.

Our Prayer: *May we still our bodies, calm our hearts, quiet our minds, empty and open our very souls, so that, unimpeded, the Holy Spirit of God may income, indwell, transform and outflow as we share God's Gifting with others.*

Read the entirety of the first lesson, exploring man's response, woman's response, God's response to them, and God's demonstration, offering a new gift to the world.

> 1. See & Perceive, Hear & Believe

Lesson 2: *Initiation: God brings his son into the world*

ISSUE. *Luke 1: 26-34* In the sixth month of Elizabeth's pregnancy, God sent the angel Gabriel to Nazareth, a town in Galilee, to a virgin pledged to be married to a man named Joseph, a descendant of David. The virgin's name was Mary. The angel went to her and said, "Greetings, you who are highly favored! The Lord is with you." Mary was greatly troubled at his words and wondered what kind of greeting this might be. But the angel said to her, "Do not be afraid, Mary; you have found favor with God. You will conceive and give birth to a son, and you are to call him Jesus. He will be great and will be called the Son of the Most High. The Lord God will give him the throne of his father David, and he will reign over Jacob's descendants forever; his kingdom will never end." "How will this be," Mary asked the angel, "since I am a virgin?"

DEMONSTRATION. *Luke 2: 4-14* So Joseph also went up from the town of Nazareth in Galilee to Judea, to Bethlehem the town of David, because he belonged to the house and line of David. He went there to register with Mary, who was pledged to be married to him and was expecting a child. While they were there, the time came for the baby to be born, and she gave birth to her firstborn, a son. She wrapped him in cloths and placed him in a manger, because there was no guest room available for them. And there were shepherds living out in the fields nearby, keeping watch over their flocks at night. An angel of the Lord appeared to them, and the glory of the Lord shone around them, and they were terrified. But the angel said to them, "Do not be afraid. I bring you good news that will cause great joy for all the people. Today in the town of David a Savior has been born to you; he is the Messiah, the Lord. This will be a sign to you: You will find a baby wrapped in cloths and lying in a manger." Suddenly a great company of the heavenly host appeared with the angel, praising God and saying, "Glory to God in the highest heaven, and on earth peace to those on whom his favor rests."

Our Reflection: *When I see and hear something amazing is going to happen, can I surrender to the process of it actually occurring?* Mary humbly submitted to God's intention for her as his servant, and then submitted to the will of her betrothed, Joseph, as he in turn submitted to God's intention that he take Mary home as his wife even though already pregnant by the Holy Spirit. This believing, having faith in God's word and following the direction of God's word, begins to define what relationship, particularly by a couple in a marriage, can be. Similarly did the Magi and shepherds, Simeon and Anna, humbly follow God's direction.

Our Prayer: *May we surrender our hearts to God's love and then surrender that faithful loving to our spouse, especially as it creates new life within us and between us, that we might submit to the world, as one.*

Read the entirety of the second lesson, exploring man's response, woman's response, God's response to them, and God's demonstration, offering a new gift to the world.

| 1. See & Perceive, Hear & Believe | + | 2. Follow |

Lesson 3: *Maturation: God's son grows in the world under God's protection*

ISSUE. *Matthew 2: 13* When they had gone, an angel of the Lord appeared to Joseph in a dream. "Get up," he said, "take the child and his mother and escape to Egypt. Stay there until I tell you, for Herod is going to search for the child to kill him."

DEMONSTRATION. *Matthew 3: 11-17* [John said] "I baptize you with water for repentance. But after me comes one who is more powerful than I, whose sandals I am not worthy to carry. He will baptize you with the Holy Spirit and fire. His winnowing fork is in his hand, and he will clear his threshing floor, gathering his wheat into the barn and burning up the chaff with unquenchable fire." Then Jesus came from Galilee to the Jordan to be baptized by John. But John tried to deter him, saying, "I need to be baptized by you, and do you come to me?" Jesus replied, "Let it be so now; it is proper for us to do this to fulfill all righteousness." Then John consented. As soon as Jesus was baptized, he went up out of the water. At that moment heaven was opened, and he saw the Spirit of God descending like a dove and alighting on him. And a voice from heaven said, "This is my Son, whom I love; with him I am well pleased."

Our Reflection: As we see, hear and surrender to the unfolding movement of God's Holy Spirit, are we comforted in the faith that God protects, promotes and realizes his plan for us? In a harsh world Joseph continued to listen to God's guidance - believing, following and having faith that God would realize the Gift he intended for the world, through Joseph and Mary's parental care of the child Jesus. We suspect that Joseph and Zachariah, Mary and Elizabeth, (as well as Simeon and Anna) would have been deeply heartened at the moment that their two sons, John and Jesus, fulfilled God's gifting in the realization that the Gift was fully initiated and confirmed by God at the baptism of Jesus. Their faithful effort over many years was validated in that moment by God. These two couples, their two children paired for a moment, were bound up for all eternity in the Father's love of His Son, seeking to nurture and bequeath a most precious gift to the world.

Our Prayer: May we continue to seek the love of God in our hearts (the-two-within-one), seek and share that faithful loving with one another (the-two-as-one), and continue to share that purely partnered love with our children and the children of others, as it creates, protects and promotes their lives in an interlinked unity with God's plan for each of them and all of them together.

Read the entirety of the third lesson, exploring man's response, woman's response, God's response to them, and God's demonstration, of sustaining this new gift to the world.

1. See & Perceive, Hear & Believe	+	2. Follow	+	3. Seek & Share

Lesson 4: *The Spiritual Testing: In the Wilderness with God, Facing Satan*

ISSUE. *Matthew 4: 1-3* Then Jesus was led by the Spirit into the wilderness to be tempted by the devil. After fasting forty days and forty nights, he was hungry. The tempter came to him and said, "If you are the Son of God, tell these stones to become bread."

DEMONSTRATION. *John 2: 1-9* On the third day a wedding took place at Cana in Galilee. Jesus' mother was there, and Jesus and his disciples had also been invited to the wedding. When the wine was gone, Jesus' mother said to him, "They have no more wine."
"Woman, why do you involve me?" Jesus replied. "My hour has not yet come."
His mother said to the servants, "Do whatever he tells you." Nearby stood six stone water jars, the kind used by the Jews for ceremonial washing, each holding from twenty to thirty gallons. Jesus said to the servants, "Fill the jars with water"; so they filled them to the brim. Then he told them, "Now draw some out and take it to the master of the banquet." They did so, and the master of the banquet tasted the water that had been turned into wine.

Our Reflection: *As we see, hear and surrender to the unfolding movement of God's Holy Spirit, can we surpass the ways we are enticed and tested toward that which is not of God and seek what is?* In a world that offers us much of pleasure, passion, wealth and worldly ambition, can we see what is only stone and water and what is truly nurturing bread and wine? Do we try to make these discernments alone, or do we partner with the words of our Lord made manifest in Holy Scripture?

Our Prayer **& Praise:** *With our bodies may we not hunger for stone, but for the bread that gives life; with our hearts may we thirst for the water that is turned into wine; with our minds may we seek not our own serpentine words but the Word that is the breath of true life; and with our souls may we empty of all but that which is of the flame of the Holy Spirit of the everlasting love of God. Lord, we praise you for helping us not only to see but to perceive, not only to hear but to believe, not to tarry but to follow your leading guidance, and not to stumble but to continue to seek you and share the gifts we find that you have shared with us, in sustaining faith and fidelity.*

Read the entirety of this fourth and final lesson of this cluster, exploring man's response, woman's response, God's response to them, and God's demonstration, of sustaining this new gift to the world.

| 1. See & Perceive, Hear & Believe | + | 2. Follow | + | 3. Seek & Share | = | 4. Faith & Fidelity |

Now, once again, read through the passages of these first four lessons, keeping in mind the bookends of 'issue' and 'demonstration', and look for themes or patterns that seem to repeat themselves. On the fourth (or fifth) week see if you can find some themes or patterns that are developed across the four lessons. Here are some motifs that seemed to pop out for us during our studies of Lessons 1-4 ...

Our Reflections on Cluster I: *Lessons 1-4*

In the book we wrote just before this one – *Small Treasures of a Human Heart: Brief Musings and Bright Illuminations of the Love Between Beauty and Truth* – we explored the nature of creation as Beauty, in all of its varied aspects. We discovered beauty comes into us, indwells and transforms us, then necessarily outflows from within us, shared outwardly with others:

1) In order to prepare for beauty we need to still the body, calm the heart, quiet the mind, empty and open the soul;

2) Attending to external beauty – the seen – we notice that at its highest quality it has *structure* ... it is plentiful, it has *function* ... it offers benefit, it has *form* ... it shares abundance, and it *frees* energy ... sustaining the fruits of intergenerational life and legacy;

3) Attaching to internal beauty – the unseen – we discovered the internalized qualities of a *humble gentleness* ... holding precious - affirming, *kindness and caring connection* ... adoring and cherishing, *considerate and compassionate contribution* ... appreciating, and a new and more *complete composition* ... revering and honoring; and finally,

4) Discerning Beauty in its fullest aspect as described in Scripture, involves integrating the seen and unseen, the external and internal, aspects of beauty by finding congruence (through dreams), permeating resonance (through visions), good fruits (through visitations of Spirit), and that the Spirit prospers (through the Word).

If all these aspects occur, we must express what has come into us, changed and transformed us – the expression of Beauty instructs the body, illuminates the heart, informs the mind, and inspires the soul. Taken together, these processes prepare for us for love, revealed ...

In the beginning of creation there were two aspects that provided a scaffold for Beauty – The Tree of the Knowledge of Good and Evil and the Tree of Everlasting Life – to the couple (Adam and Eve) who lived in that garden (Eden). The first Tree represents the perfect righteousness in response to God's Law, and the second Tree represents perfect love in response to God's Love. God warned Adam and Eve that perfect righteousness was beyond their capacity and to stay within the light of God's perfect Love. They did not and things turned quite ugly ... and terribly painful. The loss of perfect innocence could only be covered inadequately, with death. In the first instance, this was done with the skins of dead animals. Death was a consequence, not a solution, to the choice of walking outside the light of God's perfect understanding and love. The solution to this entry into darkness was for God to make explicit to Adam's descendants their incapacity to live up to God's Laws (as given to Moses) in righteousness, and to bring a single perfection of God's Love (his son, Jesus) into being in the world so that death might be overcome and the choice of once again walking into the light, out of the darkness, might be available. Righteous application of the Knowledge of Good and Evil, of the Law, can only be realized through the transcendent application of Love, illustrated perfectly by the perfect love of the Son of Man who is the Son of God, who, then, offers a successful penetration of death through his resurrection and the offer of the forgiveness and salvation through the Holy Spirit. How this penetration and resolution of the tension between the two trees, between the Law and Love, can occur, is the subject of the four Gospels. And in this first cluster of Lessons 1-4, the patterning of the nature of God's gift to us is prepared and laid out clearly.

In these first four lessons God sends angels to declare that a son (John) will be conceived and born to turn hearts and prepare people for their Lord, and a son will be conceived and born (Jesus) that will be called the Son of God, who will save his people form their sins and reign forever. The angels most often say four things again and again – 'fear not', 'a gift from God is given; rejoice', 'this is what you are to do', and 'this is what will then happen' ... all of which then occurs, involving many people and places. While some men resist (Zachariah and Herod) such truth, many men follow the provided guidance (John and Joseph, the Magi and Simeon), while all the women (Elizabeth and Mary, Anna) exhibit a rather humble trust and faith. The angel who had been the most beautiful in heaven (but who was not innocent), Satan, clearly attempts to derail what has been set in motion, but the Son does not veer from being the Father's gift – the physical manifestation of perfect knowledge and perfect good, perfect righteousness in the eyes of the Law and perfect compassion in and as the heart of Love, the revealing of pure innocence in the face of sin that dispels death and saves those souls that have been chosen by God and who have chosen God in faith.

The other patterned aspect of these first four lessons is that all is paired – Gabriel stands with God, an angel with each person, Zachariah and Elizabeth, Joseph and Mary, Simeon and Anna, Jesus and Satan, Jesus and God, Jesus and John, the killing of infants by Herod with the killing of children in Egypt, the stone and bread, water with wine, angels with light, the Holy Spirit with flame, ... and the Holy Spirit with the dove(s). As Christina and I finished our study of the first lessons in this cluster and noted these pairings, we remarked about how often a pair of doves came into Scripture. As our Bible lay open and we mentioned doves, a dove flew up and landed upon our deck railing right before us. Then another dove, its mate, flew up onto the railing beside her. They looked at us, walked around some and prepared to mate, then flew away. Pairs of doves are a symbol of the Holy Spirit and they came to us just as we were open in the Word and as we contemplated and planned for our own family ... wow!

Our Prayer & Praise: *Lord, thank you for doves. Thank you for the child now nestled inside Christina waiting to be born into our world, into our love, into your love ... already cradled in your love. Please let each of us see and perceive your love, hear and believe your love, follow your love, continue to seek and share your love, in faith and fidelity, as made manifest and embodied in the gift of your Son. As he was sent by you and is with you, may your and his love be within each of us, be shared between us. As you have gifted your child in love to the world may we gift our child to the world in your name, in your love, with your Word through the instructing, illuminating, informing inspiration of the Holy Spirit.*

Your Reflections:

Your Prayer & Praise:

Lessons 5-8

Jesus Begins Fulfilling God's Promise Through His Ministry:
Jesus Directs How to Receive God's Gift Within Each Person

5. What to believe about Jesus (John 2:23-4:54; Matt 4:12-17, 8:5-13; Mark 1:14-15; Luke 4:14-15, 7:1-10)

a. The issue: Who is Jesus?	-	Nicodemus
b. The response of man	-	John the Baptist's testimony
b. The response of woman	-	Samaritan woman
c. Jesus responds	-	I am he; living water; reaping harvest
d Jesus demonstrates	-	official's son, centurion's faith

6. Who will believe, be chosen & follow Jesus (Matt 4:18-22; Mark 1:16-20; Luke 5:1-11)

a. The issue: will you come with me?	-	walking the Sea of Galilee
b. The response of man	-	Peter, Andrew, James, John
c. Jesus response	-	put out to deep water
d. Jesus Demonstrates	-	caught fish, become fishers of men

7. The obstruction(s) to believing (Mark 1:21-38; Matt: 8:14-17, 8:2-4; Luke: 4:31-44, 5:12-16)

a. The issue: do you come to destroy?	-	demon
b. The response to Jesus presence	-	you are the Holy One of God
c. Jesus responds	-	be quiet!
d. Jesus demonstrates	-	come out of that person! Jesus heals many

8. Removing obstruction ... forgiveness and healing
(Matt 9:1-17; Mark 2:1-22; Luke 5:17-39; John 5:1-15

a. The issue: who can forgive & heal; fasting?	-	paralyzed man
b. The response by men	-	teachers of law - blasphemy
c. Jesus responds	-	Calls Matthew, eats with sinners
d. Jesus demonstrates	-	healing at the pool

First Cluster (5-8):

Pray, be born again of water & Spirit, know the gift, be quiet, open eyes & ears, see & hear, accept, believe, repent, don't entertain evil thoughts, stop sinning, be forgiven, don't be afraid, take heart, have faith, follow me, come into the light & live by the truth, be a spring of water welling up, go & learn, mercy not sacrifice, Pray

Lesson 5: *What to believe about Jesus*

ISSUE. *John 3: 1-4* Now there was a Pharisee, a man named Nicodemus who was a member of the Jewish ruling council. He came to Jesus at night and said, "Rabbi, we know that you are a teacher who has come from God. For no one could perform the signs you are doing if God were not with him." Jesus replied, "Very truly I tell you, no one can see the kingdom of God unless they are born again."
"How can someone be born when they are old?" Nicodemus asked. "Surely they cannot enter a second time into their mother's womb to be born!"

DEMONSTRATION. *Matthew 8: 5-13* When Jesus had entered Capernaum, a centurion came to him, asking for help. "Lord," he said, "my servant lies at home paralyzed, suffering terribly." Jesus said to him, "Shall I come and heal him?" The centurion replied, "Lord, I do not deserve to have you come under my roof. But just say the word, and my servant will be healed. For I myself am a man under authority, with soldiers under me. I tell this one, 'Go,' and he goes; and that one, 'Come,' and he comes. I say to my servant, 'Do this,' and he does it." When Jesus heard this, he was amazed and said to those following him, "Truly I tell you, I have not found anyone in Israel with such great faith. I say to you that many will come from the east and the west, and will take their places at the feast with Abraham, Isaac and Jacob in the kingdom of heaven. But the subjects of the kingdom will be thrown outside, into the darkness, where there will be weeping and gnashing of teeth." Then Jesus said to the centurion, "Go! Let it be done just as you believed it would." And his servant was healed at that moment.

Our Reflection*: As we come into the presence of our Lord through the Word can we truly see and hear, actually believe, that he has authority over all and everything, no matter how improbable?* In a modern world that tends to lead us to rely on mental conceptions of science and technology, believing only in the capabilities of the constructions of the expert reasoning of an educated man, can we instead lead with a deep opening of our hearts to see, hear and believe what is poured into us by a source that is above and beyond our conceptions of man-shaped and -conceived nature, to a super-natural authority that may, if it chooses, contradict our usual experiences and understandings of how things work?

In this first lesson at the very beginning of Jesus' ministry we see pairings or linking of couplets that provide us with important contrasts – light and darkness, heaven and earth, water and living water, water and Spirit, seeing signs and hearing the wind (not knowing where it comes from and not knowing where it is going), saving and condemning, signs/wonders and good news (the Word), lifting up the Son of Man and lifting up the snake, Nicodemus and the Samaritan woman, John and his disciples and Jesus and his disciples, physical food and the food of doing the will of the one who sent him, the royal official and the centurion, the son and servant of each.

Who can see and perceive accurately, who can hear and believe? The juxtaposition of Nicodemus, who is filled with the rule of law and the institutional relationships of the Sanhedrin, and the Samaritan woman, who has lived in the messy and chaotic world of love relationships with five different men, one seeking wisdom of the mind, the other presumably seeking comfort of the heart, suggests that the thirst for love is closer and more easily translated into transforming re-birth than is a thirst for knowledge and rational law. The Samaritan woman goes back to her community and shares what her heart has been opened to with resulting new believers, while nothing is said of whether Nicodemus even said anything to his fellow members of the Sanhedrin. The royal official has hope for a miracle and so he goes to see, hear and ask Jesus, after which he experiences the sign and miracle of his son being saved from death, then believing more fully. On the other hand, the Centurion has been altruistic in his community, cares about his servant without self-interest, has sufficient positive relationships with the Jews in his community to send them to Jesus for him, and understands and believes the authority of Jesus without having to see or hear it directly.

Our question is thus refined by Scripture: We ask 'who may see and hear the unseen, the unheard'? That is, while we can drink physical water, eat physical food, see and hear of signs and wonders, can we perceive that which is of heaven that only the Son of Man saw, hear the words of Jesus that come from the Father that only he heard, believe in the wind that is the Spirit from whence it comes and where it goes we know not … and how do we discern this, how do we come to believe in this invisible Spirit and sacred Silence!?!

In this lesson our sense is that it is not a single event, testimony, sign or wonder that we need to discern, but three aspects in relation to one another – the movement among what transpires previously, what transacts with the Son of God, and what happens afterwards – in other words, what inflows, indwells and outflows. So if we notice what happens before Jesus enters, what happens when the person interacts with Jesus, and then what happens afterward, we begin to experience the flow of the Holy Spirit and how it moves, translates and transforms life into re-birth.

And we realize that this text, written by different authors, including the words of Jesus and the words of others, has been inspired and arranged by the Holy Spirit, for those of us in later generations so that we might believe, not having directly seen or heard what happened two thousand years ago. So it is important to notice *how* this Sacred Text has been arranged, that in these early lessons the examples and illustrations in the text are short and simple, are paired in contrasting couplets, and lead us to a familiar four-part sequence: preparation, engaging, sharing, and then humbly praising and thanking Christ.

Our Prayer: *Let us lead with the humble receiving that comes from the greatest opening of our hearts to what we do not know, rather than the closed outflowing of what we think we know with our minds, in order that our lives might be informed and transformed … through love.*

Read the entirety of this fifth lesson of this cluster, exploring man's response, woman's response, God's response to them, and God's demonstration, of sustaining this new gift to the world.

5. Believe, Have Faith	+	6.	+	7.	=	8.

Your Reflections:

Your Prayer & Praise:

Lesson 6: *Who will believe, be chosen & follow Jesus*

ISSUE. *Luke 5: 1-5* One day as Jesus was standing by the Lake of Gennesaret, the people were crowding around him and listening to the word of God. He saw at the water's edge two boats, left there by the fishermen, who were washing their nets. He got into one of the boats, the one belonging to Simon, and asked him to put out a little from shore. Then he sat down and taught the people from the boat. When he had finished speaking, he said to Simon, "Put out into deep water, and let down the nets for a catch."
Simon answered, "Master, we've worked hard all night and haven't caught anything.

DEMONSTRATION. *Luke 5: 4-11* Then he sat down and taught the people from the boat. When he had finished speaking, he said to Simon, "Put out into deep water, and let down the nets for a catch." Simon answered, "Master, we've worked hard all night and haven't caught anything. But because you say so, I will let down the nets." When they had done so, they caught such a large number of fish that their nets began to break. So they signaled their partners in the other boat to come and help them, and they came and filled both boats so full that they began to sink. When Simon Peter saw this, he fell at Jesus' knees and said, "Go away from me, Lord; I am a sinful man!" For he and all his companions were astonished at the catch of fish they had taken, and so were James and John, the sons of Zebedee, Simon's partners. Then Jesus said to Simon, "Don't be afraid; from now on you will fish for people." So they pulled their boats up on shore, left everything and followed him.

Our Reflection: *As we see, hear and surrender to the unfolding movement of God's Holy Spirit, can we let go of all that we feel is important in our lives, heretofore, in order to follow him?* There are not only material things, but old internal habits and external relations that we have become quite accustomed to in our lives, that are like the nets, boats and family/friend ties that may keep us stuck where we are rather than where the Lord might have us go. Peter indicated to Jesus that they had worked hard all night and gotten nothing. Jesus showed him that personal efforts without the Lord that come to nothing can be transformed by the Lord into abundance and that he will have them fish for something much more important then physical food – people and their souls. In the net of Jesus are his first harvest - the souls of two pairs of brothers, in spite of Peter's protestation of being sinful. Here again we have the four-fold sequence of what happens before Jesus (hard work with no benefit), with Jesus (capturing abundance), after Jesus' response (humble prostration), and the overall culmination and continued movement (two pairs of brothers leave all and follow Jesus as disciples) of the Holy Spirit.

Our Prayer: *Lord, help us to empty ourselves and empty our lives of the attachments that unnecessarily weigh us down, burden us ... lighten our load that we might freely follow you.*

Read the entirety of this sixth lesson of this cluster, exploring man's response, woman's response, God's response to them, and God's demonstration, of sustaining this new gift to the world.

| 5. Believe, Have Faith | + | 6. Leave All, Follow | + | 7. | = | 8. |

Your Reflections:

Your Prayer & Praise:

Lesson 7: *The obstruction(s) to believing*

ISSUE. *Mark 1: 21-24* They went to Capernaum, and when the Sabbath came, Jesus went into the synagogue and began to teach. The people were amazed at his teaching, because he taught them as one who had authority, not as the teachers of the law. Just then a man in their synagogue who was possessed by an impure spirit cried out, "What do you want with us, Jesus of Nazareth? Have you come to destroy us? I know who you are—the Holy One of God!"

DEMONSTRATION. *Mark 1:29-31; Matthew 8:1-4* As soon as they left the synagogue, they went with James and John to the home of Simon and Andrew. Simon's mother-in-law was in bed with a fever, and they immediately told Jesus about her. So he went to her, took her hand and helped her up. The fever left her and she began to wait on them.

When Jesus came down from the mountainside, large crowds followed him. A man with leprosy came and knelt before him and said, "Lord, if you are willing, you can make me clean." Jesus reached out his hand and touched the man. "I am willing," he said. "Be clean!" Immediately he was cleansed of his leprosy. Then Jesus said to him, "See that you don't tell anyone. But go, show yourself to the priest and offer the gift Moses commanded, as a testimony to them."

Our Reflection: *As we faithfully believe and follow, leaving behind old material and social habits to follow the Lord's lead, can we excise those internal demons that chain us and imprison us in pain and suffering?* We may be used to altering our social systems (divorce, different friends), changing jobs and communities, but can we release and cleanse ourselves of pride, ambition, self-loathing and many other internal baggage that prevent true transformation? As Jesus exorcised and silenced the demons within the person in the synagogue, so did he cleanse the leper of his infirmity and tell him to go praise God in testimony to the priest. Once cleansed, as in the case of releasing Peter's mother-in-law of her fever after which she then waited on Jesus and his disciples, we may serve our Lord in ways that he guides and directs, through quiet listening and study (synagogue member), service (mother-in-law), testifying witness (leper), and prayer (Jesus in solitude).

Our Prayer: *Lord, as we try to still our bodies, calm our hearts, quiet our minds, empty and open our souls to you, please cleanse us so that we might be born again into a new life, with you as our constant and loving companion, serving in ways that you guide.*

Read the entirety of this seventh lesson of this cluster, exploring man's response, woman's response, God's response to them, and God's demonstration, of sustaining this new gift to the world.

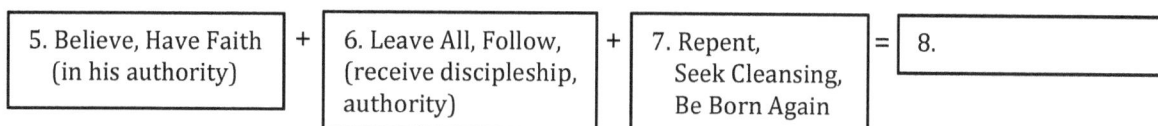

5. Believe, Have Faith (in his authority)	+	6. Leave All, Follow, (receive discipleship, authority)	+	7. Repent, Seek Cleansing, Be Born Again	=	8.

Lesson 8: *The obstruction(s) to believing*

ISSUE. *Matthew 9: 1-3* Jesus stepped into a boat, crossed over and came to his own town. Some men brought to him a paralyzed man, lying on a mat. When Jesus saw their faith, he said to the man, "Take heart, son; your sins are forgiven." At this, some of the teachers of the law said to themselves, "This fellow is blaspheming!"

DEMONSTRATION. *John 5:1-14* Some time later, Jesus went up to Jerusalem for one of the Jewish festivals. Now there is in Jerusalem near the Sheep Gate a pool, which in Aramaic is called Bethesda and which is surrounded by five covered colonnades. Here a great number of disabled people used to lie—the blind, the lame, the paralyzed. One who was there had been an invalid for thirty-eight years. When Jesus saw him lying there and learned that he had been in this condition for a long time, he asked him, "Do you want to get well?"
"Sir," the invalid replied, "I have no one to help me into the pool when the water is stirred. While I am trying to get in, someone else goes down ahead of me." Then Jesus said to him, "Get up! Pick up your mat and walk." At once the man was cured; he picked up his mat and walked…. Later Jesus found him at the temple and said to him, "See, you are well again. Stop sinning or something worse may happen to you." The man went away and told the Jewish leaders that it was Jesus who had made him well.

Our Reflection: *As we believe and have faith, leave all else, follow, repent of previous ways of being, seek cleansing and are born again into a new life, can we enter a new life after we are forgiven and sustain such a new life in Christ?* While we may change, the world may not, in the sense that the same and new temptations continually assault us, undermining the clarity of and commitment to our new life. What context do we form around us to help us sustain our faith? The contrast between a paralyzed man being brought through a crowd by his faithful friends and the longtime invalid who was alone who went to the Jewish leaders after being cured, describes the differences in being surrounded by a loving community or by a cold religious institution. In this same lesson, Jesus calls Matthew the tax collector to discipleship and eats with other such sinners, links with John's disciples asking about the lack of fasting by his disciples compared to the frequent fasting of the priests. Jesus responds that he comes for the sick not the righteous and desires mercy not sacrifice. So it is that we are to have faith, follow and repent, cleanse and be born again, stop sinning and be forgiven, but also to place ourselves in a community of faith to sustain such transformation based upon mercy and forgiveness.

Our Prayer: *Lord uplift and uphold our heart's desire for you; please provide the light of your love that enables us to see the path through the darkness that ever surrounds us, a path to sustain our faith with your ongoing forgiveness, within a solid community of faith.*

Read the entirety of this eighth and final lesson of this cluster, exploring man's response, woman's response, God's response to them, and God's demonstration, of sustaining this new gift to the world.

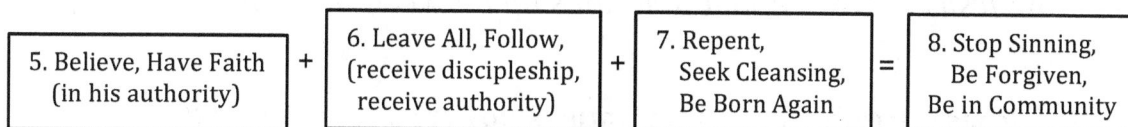

| 5. Believe, Have Faith (in his authority) | + | 6. Leave All, Follow, (receive discipleship, receive authority) | + | 7. Repent, Seek Cleansing, Be Born Again | = | 8. Stop Sinning, Be Forgiven, Be in Community |

Your Reflections:

Your Prayer & Praise:

Lessons 9-12

Jesus Shows How Each Person Should Share God's Gift With Each Other Person: *Jesus Teaches About Relationship Between One Another*

9. How Jesus is treated by men (of status & power) ... *Jesus has authority*
(John 5:16-46; Matt 12:1-14; Mark 2:23-3:6; Luke 6:1-11)

a. The issue: Is Jesus from God?   -   Jewish leaders
b. The response of men of stature   -   love of God not in your hearts
b. The response of a humble man   -   John testifies, His works testify
c. Jesus responds   -   mercy not sacrifice, do good on Sabbath
d Jesus demonstrates   -   heals shriveled hand on Sabbath

10. How some men believe, are chosen & follow Jesus ... *Jesus gives authority*
(Matt 12:15-21, 10:2-4, Acts 1;13b, Matt4:23-25; Mark 3:7-19; Luke 6:17b-18, 12-16)

a. The issue: Will you follow me?   -   fulfill Isaiah
b. The response of man   -   disciples believe, are to proclaim, preach, & teach
c. Jesus response   -   choses the disciples, gives them authority
d. Jesus Demonstrates   -   teaches in synagogues, proclaims good news, heals

11. How each person is to treat each other person ... *you have authority over your heart* (Matt 5:1-8:13; Luke 6:17a, 20-26, 29-30, 27-28, 32-36, 11:2-4, 6:37-7:10; John 4:46-54)

a. The issue: How are we to treat one another?   -   Sermon on the Mount
b. The response to Jesus presence   -   crowds follow and listen
c. Jesus responds   -   show mercy, be pure in heart, pray
d. Jesus demonstrates - centurion's faith, official's son healed, widow's dead son
                         raised

12. How each person is to rely on God and Jesus to do the above ... *your faith joins His compassion*
(Matthew 11:2-30, 26:6-13; Luke 7:18-8:3; Mark 14:3-9; John 12:1-8)

a. The issue: Is Jesus the one?   -   John's disciples
b. The response by men   -   woe be to unrepentent
c. Jesus responds   -   come to me weary & burdened, reveal to children
d. Jesus demonstrates   -   Mary washes Jesus with alabaster jar of perfume

Lesson 9: *How Jesus is treated by men (of status & power) ... Jesus has authority*

The Issue: What is lawful to do on the Sabbath; who has authority?

Man's Response: John testifies about him; Jewish leaders persecute him.

Jesus Response: God has given me works to finish; my works and Scripture (David, Moses) testify about me. God has given me authority to judge. The Son of Man is Lord of the Sabbath.

Jesus Demonstration: His disciples are fed by grains in the field; a man's shriveled hand is restored.

ISSUE. *John 5: 8-18* Then Jesus said to him, "Get up! Pick up your mat and walk." At once the man was cured; he picked up his mat and walked. The day on which this took place was a Sabbath, and so the Jewish leaders said to the man who had been healed, "It is the Sabbath; the law forbids you to carry your mat." But he replied, "The man who made me well said to me, 'Pick up your mat and walk.' " So they asked him, "Who is this fellow who told you to pick it up and walk?" The man who was healed had no idea who it was, for Jesus had slipped away into the crowd that was there. Later Jesus found him at the temple and said to him, "See, you are well again. Stop sinning or something worse may happen to you." The man went away and told the Jewish leaders that it was Jesus who had made him well. So, because Jesus was doing these things on the Sabbath, the Jewish leaders began to persecute him. In his defense Jesus said to them, "My Father is always at his work to this very day, and I too am working." For this reason they tried all the more to kill him; not only was he breaking the Sabbath, but he was even calling God his own Father, making himself equal with God.

DEMONSTRATION. *Mark 3:1-6* Another time Jesus went into the synagogue, and a man with a shriveled hand was there. Some of them were looking for a reason to accuse Jesus, so they watched him closely to see if he would heal him on the Sabbath. Jesus said to the man with the shriveled hand, "Stand up in front of everyone." Then Jesus asked them, "Which is lawful on the Sabbath: to do good or to do evil, to save life or to kill?" But they remained silent. He looked around at them in anger and, deeply distressed at their stubborn hearts, said to the man, "Stretch out your hand." He stretched it out, and his hand was completely restored. Then the Pharisees went out and began to plot with the Herodians how they might kill Jesus.

Our Reflection: We are crippled by our unbelief. We believe in the rules men have interpreted and made to judge and condemn, which obstruct and deny believing in the ongoing authority of the Father and the Son, who are life. In Lessons 5-8 we learned to empty and open, leave all behind, surrender and follow Jesus, in order to receive the Gift of God's Son, prepared and given to us in Lessons 1-4. In order to follow Him, we must believe that he has authority over all, including man's interpretations and created rules. Do persons with position, status and power have authority over us, or do we believe we can discern what God and the Son of God ask of us?

The text in this lesson pairs the Father and the Son as one, in having life and giving life, pairs John with Jesus, testifying and confirming Jesus as the Son of God, but in contrasting fashion pairs Moses and the priests, formulating that if they cannot believe their own father (Moses), how they can they believe God, the Father of Jesus? Jesus also pairs he and his disciples who are eating grains in the fields on the Sabbath, with David and his companions who ate bread in the temple, while contrasting this pairing with the fact that the priests pair with themselves, allowing them to do what is forbidden to everyone else ... for themselves. While Jesus and David feed their charges, the priests take care of themselves. Jesus points out that mercy supersedes sacrifice in the scheme of things - doing for others is better than doing for your selves. At the end of the lesson when the Pharisees ask if it is lawful to heal on the Sabbath, Jesus points out that it is ok if they will do something that benefits themselves on the Sabbath (e.g. lift a valuable sheep out of a well it has fallen into), and demonstrates it is good to do good on the Sabbath by healing the shriveled hand of a man.

It is truly amazing to perceive that Jesus concretely shows that the right hand of the Pharisees that reads Scripture, writes, interprets and expresses the Law, is deformed (shriveled), yet might be healed if they hear his voice, his word, and let his word dwell in their hearts ... that this is how to believe. Christina and I realized at this point that each demonstration of Jesus provides a direct physical manifestation of spiritual healing, within each lesson, so that we might see and perceive, hear and believe, more easily. We are awestruck at the absolute coherence in such symmetry – that physical healing of Jesus is actually, and more importantly, only a limited manifestation of a larger spiritual healing and transformation. If only the Pharisees had opened their hearts, their deformed hand of the Law might have been transformed by the heart of God's Love – mercy, not sacrifice.

Our Prayer: *Lord, let us be guided by your humble compassion, as the author of a love that surpasses man's interpretation of law, that we might empty ourselves of pride in knowledge, judgment of others, ambition, fear and anything else that might obstruct a complete opening to the simple humility of receiving your Gift.*

9. Believe God's Love Surpasses Man's rules. (He has authority.)	10.	11.	12.

Lesson 10: *How some men believe, are chosen & follow Jesus ... Jesus gives authority*

The Issue: Who is chosen to be a servant of God?

Man's Response: Many come from far places to be physically healed.

Jesus Response: Go up upon a mountain and pray to God, then choose six pairs of disciples to preach and have authority.

Jesus Demonstration: Teaching and proclaiming the good news throughout the region, Jesus heals all who come.

ISSUE. *Matthew 12: 14* But the Pharisees went out and plotted how they might kill Jesus.

DEMONSTRATION. *Luke 6:12-13; Matthew 10: 2-4; Matthew 5: 23-25* One of those days Jesus went out to a mountainside to pray, and spent the night praying to God. When morning came, he called his disciples to him and chose twelve of them, whom he also designated apostles: ... first, Simon (who is called Peter) and his brother Andrew; James son of Zebedee, and his brother John; Philip and Bartholomew; Thomas and Matthew the tax collector; James son of Alphaeus, and Thaddaeus; Simon the Zealot and Judas Iscariot, who betrayed him. Jesus went throughout Galilee, teaching in their synagogues, proclaiming the good news of the kingdom, and healing every disease and sickness among the people. News about him spread all over Syria, and people brought to him all who were ill with various diseases, those suffering severe pain, the demon-possessed, those having seizures, and the paralyzed; and he healed them. Large crowds from Galilee, the Decapolis, Jerusalem, Judea and the region across the Jordan followed him.

Our Reflection: While the Pharisees sought to kill him and his message, huge crowds followed him in hopes of physical healing. Yet his concern was for their spiritual transformation and re-birth ... so he chose 12 to go forth in his name to serve this intent. As these six pairs were chosen and given authority to love in the manner Jesus loved, even now one must be chosen by the Father and the Son to be a servant, for the in-dwelling of his words to create and be given authority to heal physically and spiritually. For in those who empty, open, leave all else, follow, and believe in his authority, then his love, delight and hope will dwell within, as each sees and hears the Word in his/her heart.

Our Prayer: *Lord, as you chose who would receive discipleship and authority of your Holy Spirit, let the Gift of your Spirit make disciples and apostles of us.*

9. Believe God's Love Surpasses Man's rules. (He has authority.)	10. Leave All, Follow, (receive discipleship, receive authority)	11.	12

Lesson 11: *He is the Son of God, the Bread of Life (you have authority over your heart)*

The Issue: How are we to receive the Gift of the Son of God into our hearts?

Man's Response: Succumb to our terrible conditions and circumstances; give in to our negative impulses; follow false prophets; worry and come to despair.

Jesus Response: Sermon on the Mount – the what, how and why of receiving the Gift of the Son from God.

Jesus Demonstration: Healing the centurion's servant; raising a widow's son from the dead.

ISSUE: *Matthew 4:11* ... people insult you, persecute you and falsely say all kinds of evil against you because of me.

DEMONSTRATION: *Luke 7: 11-17* Soon afterward, Jesus went to a town called Nain, and his disciples and a large crowd went along with him. As he approached the town gate, a dead person was being carried out—the only son of his mother, and she was a widow. And a large crowd from the town was with her. When the Lord saw her, his heart went out to her and he said, "Don't cry." Then he went up and touched the bier they were carrying him on, and the bearers stood still. He said, "Young man, I say to you, get up!" The dead man sat up and began to talk, and Jesus gave him back to his mother. They were all filled with awe and praised God. "A great prophet has appeared among us," they said. "God has come to help his people." This news about Jesus spread throughout Judea and the surrounding country.

Our Reflection: The Sermon on the Mount gives detailed directions about how to view our condition and circumstances, what attitudes and actions we can have towards ourselves and others, why and what we are and what we should do, and how orienting are hearts toward God enables us to do these things, to be this way:

1) *What you are and what your condition is, is already blessed ...*

Matthew 5: 1-12 He said:

Blessed are the poor in spirit, for theirs is the kingdom of heaven.
Blessed are those who mourn, for they will be comforted.
Blessed are the meek, for they will inherit the earth.
Blessed are those who hunger and thirst for righteousness, for they will be filled.
Blessed are the merciful, for they will be shown mercy.
Blessed are the pure in heart, for they will see God.
Blessed are the peacemakers, for they will be called children of God.
Blessed are those who are persecuted because of righteousness, for theirs is the kingdom of heaven.
Blessed are you when people insult you, persecute you and falsely say all kinds of

evil against you because of me. Rejoice and be glad, because great is your reward in heaven, for in the same way they persecuted the prophets who were before you.

2) *How your attitudes, feelings, impulses and responses toward yourself and others - within yourself - should be, should not assert against, but affirm ...*

Matthew 5: 17-48; 7: 1-6

- do not be angry	+ reconcile, settle differences quickly
- do not lust	+ throw it away
- do not swear oaths	+ say yes or no
- do not resist a slap	+ turn the other cheek
- if they take what is yours	+ give them more
- if they force you to go	+ go further
- if they ask to borrow	+ do not turn away
- if they are your enemies	+ love and pray for them
- do not notice other's fault	+ focus on your own
- do not judge	+ forgive
- do not give dogs what is sacred	+ give to those with open hearts

3) *Why and what you are and should do, within your own heart, is ...*

Matthew 5: 13-16; 7: 7-12
You are the salt of the earth.
You are the light of the world.
Let your light shine before others, that they may see your good deeds and glorify your Father in heaven.

Ask and it will be given to you;
seek and you will find;
knock and the door will be opened to you.
In everything, do to others what you would have them do to you, for this sums up the Law and the Prophets.

4) *All is this: Orient what is in your heart toward God ...*

Matthew 6: 1-15
Do not to practice your righteousness in front of others to be seen by them.
When you give to the needy, do not announce it with trumpets, as the hypocrites do.
When you give to the needy, do not let your left hand know what your right hand is doing.

"And when you pray, do not be like the hypocrites to be seen by others,
When you pray, go into your room, close the door and pray to your Father, who is unseen.
When you pray, do not keep on babbling. This, is how you should pray:

"'Our Father in heaven, hallowed be your name,
your kingdom come, your will be done, on earth as it is in heaven.
Give us today our daily bread.
And forgive us our debts, as we also have forgiven our debtors.
And lead us not into temptation, but deliver us from the evil one."

Forgive other people when they sin against you.
When you fast, do not look somber as the hypocrites do.
When you fast, put oil on your head and wash your face, so that it will not be
obvious to others that you are fasting.

Do not store up for yourselves treasures on earth.
Store up for yourselves treasures in heaven.
For where your treasure is, there your heart will be also.

The eye is the lamp of the body. If your eyes are healthy, your whole body will be full
of light. But if your eyes are unhealthy, your whole body will be full of darkness.

"No one can serve two masters. You cannot serve both God and money.

Do not worry about your life, what you will eat or drink; or about your body, what
you will wear.
Seek first his kingdom and his righteousness, and all these things will be given to
you as well. Therefore do not worry about tomorrow, for tomorrow will worry
about itself. Each day has enough trouble of its own.

Point and Principle: For in those who empty, open, leave all else, follow, believe in
his authority, are chosen by the Father and the Son to be a servant, and those who
his love dwells within sees and hears the word in his/her heart. Then, in this
progression ...

> + *What you are and what your condition is, is already blessed;*
> + *How your attitudes, feelings, impulses and responses should be toward yourself*
>   *and others - within your self - should not assert against others, but affirm them;*
> + *Why and what you are and should do, within your own heart, is light glorifying;*
> + *All is this: Orient what is in your heart toward God.*

This brings us back to the centurion and how his faith in Jesus brought to him the
healing for his servant that he sought. Yet, the final demonstration in this lesson
goes beyond faith and beyond death. Even unsought, Jesus had compassion for the
widow who had lost her son and raises her son from death, giving life even after
death, in spite of death.

| 9. *Believe* God's Love Surpasses Man's rules. (He has authority.) | 10. Leave All, *Follow,* (He gives authority: receive discipleship, receive authority) | 11. Repent, *Seek* Cleansing, Be Born Again (You have authority and choice over your own heart - love everyone as I have loved you) | 12. |

Lesson 12: *Faith and His Compassion Gives Life (it is what is in your heart, not your mind that welcomes what is needed and supplied)*

The Issue: Is this really the Gift of God, His Son?

Man's/Woman's Response: Questioning the actions of Jesus; Anointing Jesus with tears and oil.

Jesus Response: Sermon on the Mount – the what, how and why of receiving the Gift of the Son from God.

Jesus Demonstration: Forgiveness of the woman's sins.

ISSUE: *Matthew 11: 2-3* When John, who was in prison, heard about the deeds of the Messiah, he sent his disciples to ask him, "Are you the one who is to come, or should we expect someone else?"

DEMONSTRATION: *Matthew 11: 4- 6; Luke 7: 36-50* Jesus replied, "Go back and report to John what you hear and see: The blind receive sight, the lame walk, those who have leprosy are cleansed, the deaf hear, the dead are raised, and the good news is proclaimed to the poor. Blessed is anyone who does not stumble on account of me."

When one of the Pharisees invited Jesus to have dinner with him, he went to the Pharisee's house and reclined at the table. A woman in that town who lived a sinful life learned that Jesus was eating at the Pharisee's house, so she came there with an alabaster jar of perfume. As she stood behind him at his feet weeping, she began to wet his feet with her tears. Then she wiped them with her hair, kissed them and poured perfume on them. When the Pharisee who had invited him saw this, he said to himself, "If this man were a prophet, he would know who is touching him and what kind of woman she is—that she is a sinner." Jesus answered him, "Simon, I have something to tell you." "Tell me, teacher," he said.
"Two people owed money to a certain moneylender. One owed him five hundred denarii, and the other fifty. Neither of them had the money to pay him back, so he forgave the debts of both. Now which of them will love him more?" Simon replied, "I suppose the one who had the bigger debt forgiven."
"You have judged correctly," Jesus said. Then he turned toward the woman and said to Simon, "Do you see this woman? I came into your house. You did not give me any water for my feet, but she wet my feet with her tears and wiped them with her hair. You did not give me a kiss, but this woman, from the time I entered, has not stopped kissing my feet. You did not put oil on my head, but she has poured perfume on my feet. Therefore, I tell you, her many sins have been forgiven—as her great love has shown. But whoever has been forgiven little loves little." Then Jesus said to her, "Your sins are forgiven." The other guests began to say among themselves, "Who is this who even forgives sins?" Jesus said to the woman, "Your faith has saved you; go in peace."

Our Reflection: Those who empty and open, follow, believe, are chosen and in whom his love indwells, see and hear his word in their hearts. What happens, then, in this progression, is that belief becomes love and love becomes faith. As the inflowing of God's love, into that sacred space within the human heart that has been cleared of all worldly debris, fills with his love and fulfills his word, we fall into that love and that love overflows and outflows from our hearts in joyful surrender and glory. It is within this lovely flow that we repent and are forgiven, as our love grows into an ever-maturing faith.

And it is this that surpasses even the authority over death – that our sins may be forgiven so we might be re-born spiritually and be gifted with eternal life within his compassionate love.

Our Prayer: *Lord, we believe, we follow, we seek to offer the love you have offered to us, and we humbly embrace your forgiveness and share that forgiveness with others; please help us to do these things beyond our imperfect human capacity, as the very precious gift of love you created each of us to be, within the glory of the perfect love that you are.*

9. *Believe* God's Love Surpasses Man's rules. (He has authority.)	10. Leave All, *Follow*, (He gives authority: receive discipleship, receive authority)	11. Repent, *Seek* Cleansing, Be Born Again (You have authority and choice over your own heart - love everyone as I have loved you)	12. Stop Sinning, Be Forgiven, (Allow and enable others to be forgiven within the encompassing love of God and compassion of Christ ... praise the Lord for doing so.)

Lessons 13-16

Jesus Shows How Sharing God's Gift with various Groups Goes:
Jesus Teaches About Relations with Family, Groups & Communities

13. How Jesus is treated by family and different groups
(Matt 12:22-13:53, 8:18,23-34, 9:18-34; Mark 3:20-5:43; Luke11:14-23, 8:19-21,8:4-18, 8:4:22-56)

a. The issue: Is Jesus Son of David or Beelzebul? - Pharisees, teachers of law
b. The response of Jesus family - he is out of his mind
c. Jesus responds - 7 more demons replace, sower, lamp, growing, mustard
d Jesus demonstrates - calms storm, restores man/pigs, raises dead girl, heals

14. Approaching councils & communities
(Matt 13:54-58, 9:35-10:32; Mark 6:1-7, 6:16-19, 6:8-11; Luke 4:16-9:5)

a. The issue: Where did wisdom of Jesus come from? - Hometown Nazareth
b. The response of community - offense, without honor in hometown
c. Jesus response - workers are few
d. Jesus demonstrates- sends out Twelve in pairs, authority to heal, dust feet

15. The rule of law or the will of God (that is the Bread of Life, who is Jesus)
(Matt 11:1, 14:1-36; Mark 6:12-56; Luke 9:6-9, 3:19-20, 9:10-17; John6:1-71)

a. The issue: Is Jesus Elijah, John raised form dead? - Herod
b. The response the ruler - behead John the Baptist
c. Jesus responds - withdraws, preaches to crowd
d. Jesus demonstrates - feeds 5,000, walks on water, Jesus is bread of life

16. What comes out of the heart is most important   (Matt 15:1-39; Mark 7;1-8:10)

a. The issue: Who breaks commands, defiles?- Pharisees & teachers of the law
b. The response by men - eating with unwashed hands defiles
c. Jesus responds - it is what comes out, not what goes in that defiles
d. Jesus demonstrates - heals Canaanite woman & deaf man, feeds 4,000

Lessons 13-16

Jesus Shows How Sharing God's Gift with various Groups Goes:
Jesus teaches about <u>relations among</u> family, groups & communities.

13. How Jesus is treated by family and different groups
14. Approaching councils & communities
15. The rule of law or the will of God (that is the Bread of Life, who is Jesus)
16. What comes out of the heart is most important

Lesson 13: *He Has Authority (over what obstructs seeing, hearing, speaking what is healthy and whole ... removes fear to make room for faith)*

ISSUE. *Mathew 12: 22-28* Then they brought him a demon-possessed man who was blind and mute, and Jesus healed him, so that he could both talk and see. All the people were astonished and said, "Could this be the Son of David?"

But when the Pharisees heard this, they said, "It is only by Beelzebul, the prince of demons, that this fellow drives out demons." Jesus knew their thoughts and said to them, "Every kingdom divided against itself will be ruined, and every city or household divided against itself will not stand. If Satan drives out Satan, he is divided against himself. How then can his kingdom stand? And if I drive out demons by Beelzebul, by whom do your people drive them out? So then, they will be your judges. But if it is by the Spirit of God that I drive out demons, then the kingdom of God has come upon you.

DEMONSTRATION. *Matthew 8: 26, 30-32; 9: 20-32* He replied, "You of little faith, why are you so afraid?" Then he got up and rebuked the winds and the waves, and it was completely calm. Some distance from them a large herd of pigs was feeding. The demons begged Jesus, "If you drive us out, send us into the herd of pigs. "He said to them, "Go!" So they came out and went into the pigs, and the whole herd rushed down the steep bank into the lake and died in the water. Just then a woman who had been subject to bleeding for twelve years came up behind him and touched the edge of his cloak. She said to herself, "If I only touch his cloak, I will be healed." Jesus turned and saw her. "Take heart, daughter," he said, "your faith has healed you." And the woman was healed at that moment. When Jesus entered the synagogue leader's house and saw the noisy crowd and people playing pipes, he said, "Go away. The girl is not dead but asleep." But they laughed at him. After the crowd had been put outside, he went in and took the girl by the hand, and she got up. News of this spread through all that region. As Jesus went on from there, two blind men followed him, calling out, "Have mercy on us, Son of David!" When he had gone indoors, the blind men came to him, and he asked them, "Do you believe that I am able to do this?"

"Yes, Lord," they replied. Then he touched their eyes and said, "According to your faith let it be done to you"; and their sight was restored. Jesus warned them sternly,

"See that no one knows about this." But they went out and spread the news about him all over that region.

While they were going out, a man who was demon-possessed and could not talk was brought to Jesus. And when the demon was driven out, the man who had been mute spoke.

<u>Our Reflection:</u> The issue is clearly stated by Jesus in terms of a family, household, community, city or kingdom divided cannot stand, illustrated by his family thinking him out of his mind and the teachers of the law suggesting he is possessed by Beezebul. Jesus emphasizes this challenge of 'who can see and hear with understanding the kingdom of God' by casting out a demon out of a blind and mute man, so that he might see and speak of what he sees and hears. In this short thirteenth lesson, Jesus then goes on to tell parables or very brief narratives – what we will call *little stories* – to illuminate the nature of this challenge for disciples and would-be-believers who would follow him. If our perception of a 4 x 4 pattern holds, we might try to cluster these little stories into four separate sequences, each containing four basic elements ...

1) kingdom divided – strong man's house – calloused hearts and impure spirits return – Jonah/Nineveh, Solomon/Queen of the South and the three days/nights of Jesus

In the end, you cannot have both light and darkness, good and evil inhabit the same space; each person and community must decide what is good to hold on to and what is bad to expel.

2) Hidden treasure in field – pearl – owners storeroom – lamp on a stand

The treasure must be found, valued, protected and, finally, displayed, for all to see.

3) sown seeds -- growing seed -- mustard seed – seeds and weeds

This treasure, sown on good soil as seeds, will grow to abundance and be harvested separately from what is worthless.

4) yeast – good/bad tree and its fruit – netted fish sorted by good/bad – demon
filled pigs die

Unseen yeast (good or bad spirit stuff) is worked all through the dough (person) and then what (the heart) of a tree is full of will produce good or bad fruit, just as the net catches all but what is of value and what is not (in a family or community) is sorted out, and the bad that is thrown away (into pigs) falls into a great emptiness and is destroyed.

Simply put, we must be able to see, hear, accept and believe that good and evil exit in ourselves, our families and communities; we must follow our discernment and treasure what is most valuable, letting it grow in us until it bears fruit and (additional seed), seek good soil where that treasure (seed) might be shared (planted) beneficially with our partners, families, groups and communities, so that there is a plentiful harvest (fruit).

In the demonstrative healings of Jesus the text again moves us through opening our eyes and voices, repenting and casting out demons (from four men), showing what faith can accomplish (bleeding woman), and showing authority over death (raising girl). Jesus chastises the disciples for their lack of faith and teaches them that they will soon face stormy waters when he shortly sends them out into communities to do what he has done.

Our Prayer: *Lord, there is darkness and evil all around me, but the light of your love is the treasure, the pearl, the seed of new life that is growing abundantly in my heart; please water it well with the nourishment of your Holy Spirit, so that I might bear good fruit and seed to be planted in the good soil you guide me to find, that I may garden such new plantings, such new life, re-born of the seeds of your abundant love, so that you will have much of value to harvest it the season as it ends.*

13. See, hear, believe (discern what is good and safeguard it)	14.	15.	16.

Lesson 14: Approaching councils & communities: *He Gives Authority*

ISSUE. *Matthew 13: 54-58* Coming to his hometown, he began teaching the people in their synagogue, and they were amazed. "Where did this man get this wisdom and these miraculous powers?" they asked. "Isn't this the carpenter's son? Isn't his mother's name Mary, and aren't his brothers James, Joseph, Simon and Judas? Aren't all his sisters with us? Where then did this man get all these things?" And they took offense at him. But Jesus said to them, "A prophet is not without honor except in his own town and in his own home." And he did not do many miracles there because of their lack of faith.

DEMONSTRATION. *Matthew 10: 1-4; Mark 6:* Jesus called his twelve disciples to him and gave them authority to drive out impure spirits and to heal every disease and sickness. These are the names of the twelve apostles: first, Simon (who is called Peter) and his brother Andrew; James son of Zebedee, and his brother John; Philip and Bartholomew; Thomas and Matthew the tax collector; James son of Alphaeus, and Thaddaeus; Simon the Zealot and Judas Iscariot, who betrayed him. Calling the Twelve to him, he began to send them out two by two and gave them authority over impure spirits.

Our Reflection: There are four parts to sending out disciples as apostles ... 1) He brings not peace but a sword of belief that will separate man from his father, daughter from her mother, daughter-in-law from her mother-in-law and make enemies of those in the same household. 2) His harvesting sword is borne by few workers who he sends out two by two, in pairs, with the directives – do not be afraid, you will be given what to say, proclaim from the roofs, speak in the daylight, dusting off feet when not welcome and flee to other places when persecuted, acknowledging me before others. 3) Local councils will flog, governors and kings will persecute, and spreading the good news will cause brother and brother, father and child, children and parents, to betray one another unto death. 4) Freely you have received, freely give; anyone who welcomes you, welcomes me and anyone who welcome me welcomes the one who sent me; whoever loses their life, will find it.

Our Prayer: Lord, in the turbulent waters of a world frothing with good and evil, strengthen our faith to follow your footsteps, going forth with a clear voice to offer other the good news to those who would believe and follow in turn.

13. See, hear, believe (discern what is good and safeguard it)	14. Leave All, Follow, (receive & seed/share discipleship, authority)	15.	16.

Lesson 15: *He is the Son of God, the Bread of Life* *(he supplies, uplifts, upholds)*

ISSUE. *Matthew 11: 1-3, 14: 1-2* After Jesus had finished instructing his twelve disciples, he went on from there to teach and preach in the towns of Galilee. When John, who was in prison, heard about the deeds of the Messiah, he sent his disciples to ask him, "Are you the one who is to come, or should we expect someone else?"

At that time Herod the tetrarch heard the reports about Jesus, and he said to his attendants, "This is John the Baptist; he has risen from the dead! That is why miraculous powers are at work in him."

DEMONSTRATION. *Matthew 14: 16-33* Jesus replied, "They do not need to go away. You give them something to eat."
"We have here only five loaves of bread and two fish," they answered.
"Bring them here to me," he said. And he directed the people to sit down on the grass. Taking the five loaves and the two fish and looking up to heaven, he gave thanks and broke the loaves. Then he gave them to the disciples, and the disciples gave them to the people. They all ate and were satisfied, and the disciples picked up twelve basketfuls of broken pieces that were left over. The number of those who ate was about five thousand men, besides women and children. Immediately Jesus made the disciples get into the boat and go on ahead of him to the other side, while he dismissed the crowd. After he had dismissed them, he went up on a mountainside by himself to pray. Later that night, he was there alone, and the boat was already a considerable distance from land, buffeted by the waves because the wind was against it.

Shortly before dawn Jesus went out to them, walking on the lake. When the disciples saw him walking on the lake, they were terrified. "It's a ghost," they said, and cried out in fear. But Jesus immediately said to them: "Take courage! It is I. Don't be afraid."

"Lord, if it's you," Peter replied, "tell me to come to you on the water."
"Come," he said.
Then Peter got down out of the boat, walked on the water and came toward Jesus. But when he saw the wind, he was afraid and, beginning to sink, cried out, "Lord, save me!" Immediately Jesus reached out his hand and caught him. "You of little faith," he said, "why did you doubt?" And when they climbed into the boat, the wind died down. Then those who were in the boat worshiped him, saying, "Truly you are the Son of God."

Our Reflection: John the Baptist has lit the way for the true light and his job is almost done … almost done, except that his being killed by the ruler of the region and placed in a tomb foreshadows what happens to Jesus, and, eventually, to most of the disciples – they will be rejected, persecuted and killed by the institutional leaders of their time.

This is the second time that Jesus has sent his disciples out away from him, ahead of him. In what happens next, Jesus moves from a focus upon what *was* (prophesied) and what *is* (the fulfillment in healing and miracles), to what *will be* (a new portal and path to eternal life).

The flesh and blood of Jesus walks above the land and now also walks above the water, showing the disciples that His Flesh and Blood is Spirit (-in-flesh). To move with and in Spirit there must be faith and Peter's request to move to and with Jesus, above the land and water falters when his eyes move to the wind and waves and fear replaces faith. Yet, Jesus shows Peter and all the disciples that while he sends them out apart from Him, He will always return to them and will lift them up from certain death by wind and water and land beneath the stormy waves ... they need only reach out for Him, replacing fear with faith, and He will lift up their spirit with His Spirit.

This sending forth of the disciples, coming back to them and lifting up from death, out of fear, into faith, by the flesh and blood Jesus, foreshadows the third time he will send them out and leave them to return again fully as Spirit. The Holy Spirit is placed directly into their hearts, never to leave them again, until Spirit becomes Spirit when they leave their own flesh and blood and join the risen Christ in heaven.

So this walking upon the waters is *between* – it bridges, the sharing of bread the previous day and the spilling of His Blood yet to come. His next words the following day lay this out clearly, in voicing that hunger and thirst for the Spirit is what will be more importantly quenched, in the eating of his flesh and the drinking of his blood yet to come.

Here again we have this very specific linking of physical demonstration – in this case feeding of the multitudes – and spiritual provision – it will be the offering of his flesh and blood (bread and wine) that will nourish the souls of those who will be saved in eternity.

Our Prayer: *Lord, in the drought-stricken land of a starving and thirst-stricken world desiccated by evil, deepen our capacity to see the unseen spiritual provision that will feed the hunger and quench the thirst of our souls for eternity.*

13. See, hear, believe (discern what is good and safeguard it)	14. Leave All, Follow, (receive & seed/share discipleship, authority)	15. *Seek & share* spiritual cleansing, re-birth, spread (forgive, harvest souls)	16.

Lesson 16: *Faith and His Compassion Gives Life (it is what is in your heart, not your mind that welcomes what is needed and supplied)*

ISSUE. *Matthew 15: 1-2; Mark 7: 6-7* Then some Pharisees and teachers of the law came to Jesus from Jerusalem and asked, "Why do your disciples break the tradition of the elders? They don't wash their hands before they eat!" He replied, "Isaiah was right when he prophesied about you hypocrites; as it is written:
"'These people honor me with their lips, but their hearts are far from me.
They worship me in vain; their teachings are merely human rules."

DEMONSTRATION. *Matthew 15: 21-38* Leaving that place, Jesus withdrew to the region of Tyre and Sidon. A Canaanite woman from that vicinity came to him, crying out, "Lord, Son of David, have mercy on me! My daughter is demon-possessed and suffering terribly."Jesus did not answer a word. So his disciples came to him and urged him, "Send her away, for she keeps crying out after us." He answered, "I was sent only to the lost sheep of Israel."
The woman came and knelt before him. "Lord, help me!" she said.
He replied, "It is not right to take the children's bread and toss it to the dogs."
"Yes it is, Lord," she said. "Even the dogs eat the crumbs that fall from their master's table." Then Jesus said to her, "Woman, you have great faith! Your request is granted." And her daughter was healed at that moment.

Jesus left there and went along the Sea of Galilee. Then he went up on a mountainside and sat down. Great crowds came to him, bringing the lame, the blind, the crippled, the mute and many others, and laid them at his feet; and he healed them. The people were amazed when they saw the mute speaking, the crippled made well, the lame walking and the blind seeing. And they praised the God of Israel. Jesus called his disciples to him and said, "I have compassion for these people; they have already been with me three days and have nothing to eat. I do not want to send them away hungry, or they may collapse on the way."His disciples answered, "Where could we get enough bread in this remote place to feed such a crowd?"
"How many loaves do you have?" Jesus asked.
"Seven," they replied, "and a few small fish."
He told the crowd to sit down on the ground. Then he took the seven loaves and the fish, and when he had given thanks, he broke them and gave them to the disciples, and they in turn to the people. They all ate and were satisfied. Afterward the disciples picked up seven basketfuls of broken pieces that were left over. The number of those who ate was four thousand men, besides women and children.

Our Reflection: Here is the shift in the ministry of Jesus, from a local focus on the Jews of Israel to a more inclusive healing and saving of the Gentiles of other nations. Here again we have the physical healing of crippled and lame, blind and mute, followed by the compassion of Jesus feeding the multitudes. This feeding of thousands represents an inseparable physical and spiritual nourishing of people in all nations. Once cleansed of the staggering array of sicknesses, diseases and demons carried by human beings, the spiritual pouring in and over receptive souls occurs, saving these souls for his Father, for eternity.

Our Prayer: *Lord, in the drought-stricken land of a starving and thirst-stricken world desiccated by evil, deepen our capacity to see the unseen spiritual provision that will feed the hunger and quench the thirst of our souls for eternity and provision us with the words and acts that will share this gift of salvation with others, through faith in Your Compassion and Grace.*

13. See, hear, *believe* (discern what is good and safeguard it)	14. Leave All, *Follow*, (receive & seed/share discipleship, authority)	15. *Seek & share* spiritual cleansing, re-birth, spread (seek to harvest souls)	16. Sin no more, Be Forgiven, (Enable others to be forgiven & saved through *faith.*)

Your Reflections:

Your Prayer & Praise:

Sixteen Stories in Lessons 11-13

SEE :: *The treasure must be found, valued, protected, paid for, and, finally, displayed, for all to see Where treasure lies there is the heart* :: **BELIEVE**

13.10 Hidden treasure in field – [kingdom of heaven, found it, hid it, sold all he had
for it]
13.11 pearl – [kingdom of heaven, found one of great value, sold everything for it]
11.1 treasures on earth moths & vermin   13.12 owners storeroom – [in heaven,
where your treasure is there your heart is also][brings out new and old treasures]
11.2 eyes lamp of the body under a bowl   13.6 lamp on a stand   house on a hill
[let your light shine before others, giving light to everyone that they may see your
good deeds and glorify your Father in Heaven]

HEAR :: *This treasure, sown on good soil as seeds, will grow to abundance and be harvested separately from what is worthless* :: **FOLLOW** *(do likewise)*

13.5 sown seeds – [seed is the word of God, hears it understands and produces a
good crop]
13.7 growing seed – [kingdom of God]
13.9 mustard seed – [kingdom of heaven]
13.8 seeds and weeds [kingdom of heaven like a man who sowed good seed in a field
of good soil which is one who hears the word and understands it]

EMPTY & OPEN (repent) :: *light & darkness, good & evil may inhabit the same space; what is good hold, what is bad expel* :: **SEEK & SECURE** (have faith ... in the word)

11.10 wise builds on rock
13.2 strong man's house –
13.1 kingdom divided –
13.4 calloused hearts and impure spirits return –

BE GOOD FRUIT :: **LOVE** *The unseen is worked all through the heart producing fruit; what is of value or not is sorted and the bad is destroyed* :: **LIVE ETERNALLY**

13.10 yeast of the woman–   16.1 yeast of the Pharisees salt of the earth
11.8-10 wolves in sheep's clothing; good/bad tree fruit; grapes thistles, figs
thornbushes
14.1 as sheep among wolves be shrewd as snakes and innocent as doves
13.13 netted fish sorted by good/bad –
23. 7 fig tree cut down 11.6 Good gifts to children bread stone, fish snake

[*lesson number.number of stories in that lesson*] ... 11.10 = the tenth story in Lesson Eleven]

Finding the Treasure

In this first cluster of four little stories about the treasure that is the kingdom of heaven, the first story starts with a man who happened to find the treasure in a field and hid it again, then he went and bought the field in his joy. The second story involves someone more informed and knowledgeable – a merchant – who knows what he is looking for and eventually finds it, then goes far beyond the man in the first story by selling everything he had and buying it. The third story significantly extends the first two by beginning to suggest what the nature of the treasure is: It is of the heart, where it is best stored, in heaven not on earth, and then makes the pointed prediction of what happens if your treasure is of the earth and stored there – vermin and moths will destroy or thieves will break in and steal the treasure. Finally, the fourth story shows that if you can find the treasure, bring it home to your heart and secure it against destruction or loss, then it may be shared as a shining light for others to see, be comforted by, and to welcome into their own hearts, as a beacon for the treasure they may seek, find, purchase, store and share. (And in an associated story of a very informed disciple of the kingdom of heaven - a teacher of the law - the owner of the house of light may bring out of his storeroom both old and new treasures ... treasures of the old covenant of law and the new covenant of love.)

Sharing the Treasure

In the second cluster of four little stories, the treasure has been identified and condensed into its most concentrated form – a seed that is the word of God. In the first story the placement by the sower of these little seeds that have such great potential is most relevant and important – if placed on a path, on rocky soil or among thorns, the seed or young plant is destroyed – it only has a chance to survive if it is placed on good, protected, fertile soil. The second story describes the next phase in an unusual way – the seed in the soil now grows, sprouts and produces grain – without the man who scattered the seeds knowing how this happens, night and day, whether he is wake or asleep, suggesting that there is something mysterious within the soil and within the seed and plant that miraculously promotes this to happen. The third story characterizes the kingdom of heaven as the smallest of seeds, the mustard seed, that grows into the largest of garden plants, and that when it becomes a tree, many come to perch, rest and be fed. And the fourth story in this cluster completes the sequence by telling of one who sows weeds among the good seeds planted in the field and how the weeds grow alongside the wheat and cannot be entirely removed without destroying the good crop, but must be sorted and thrown into the fire at the time of harvesting the abundant grain that was originally planted by the sower, the owner of the land. Thus, we have a sequence of planting seed, growing, maturing and harvesting.

Storing and Securing the Treasure

In the third cluster of four little stories, the focus shifts to the home for the light and the seed, that which houses the treasure that has been found, planted and harvested within a person, family household, or small community. In the first little story we are cautioned to locate and build our house upon a solid foundation – rock (the word) rather than sand – so that the inevitable rains and winds may not sweep the home away. The second story very briefly suggests that once the foundation is laid, that a person must be strong so that no one might carry off the person's possessions; that might only be done if the strong person was somehow tied up. This being tied up scenario is described in the third little story about Satan's house divided against itself cannot stand, that we must gather together with the Son of God or be scattered. And in the final little story, we are told that even if we expel the impure spirit from our heart that is our home, sweep it clean and put it in order, without filling it with the light and word of the Holy Spirit, seven more impure spirits may come to the vacant home and occupy it.

Harvesting the Treasure

In the fourth and final cluster of four little stories, the battle between light and darkness, the challenge of finding and holding on to the treasure, that is the seed (the word), that is the kingdom of heaven, is truly enjoined and completed. In the first little story the yeast of a woman (cherishing what is dear) is contrasted with the yeast of the Pharisees (hypocrisy), both of which may come to permeate through and through a person, household or community. In the second little story we find that although discriminating between sheep and wolves in sheep's clothing may be difficult, we are to go out as lambs among wolves, shrewd as snakes but as innocent as doves, in order to spread the seed of light through the word to others. In the third little story we are told that figs do not grow on thornbushes or grapes on thistles and good fruit does not come from bad trees, that therefore we must not give stones but give bread to our children, not give them snakes but fish, so that they might grow into good trees bearing good fruit. In the fourth story, the outcome is made clear as the fig tree is cut down when it does not produce good fruit and bad fish are sorted from the good fish and thrown away ... eventually harvesting occurs.

Lessons 17-20

Jesus Shows that God's Gift of the Messiah Provides the Path to Heaven for Some:
Jesus Teaches About the Kingdom of Heaven and how reaching it may be Obstructed

17. The understanding & faith of the Disciples   (Matt 16:1-12 Mark 8:11-26)

a. The issue: Do you understand, have faith?   -   Disciples
b. The response of Pharisees & Sadducees   -   show a sign from heaven
c. Jesus responds   -   guard against yeast of Pharisees & Sadducees
d Jesus demonstrates   -   heals blind man's sight

18. Jesus recognized as Messiah, Savior by Disciples
(Matt 16:13-17:13; Mark 8:27-13; Luke 9:18-36)

a. The issue: Who do the crowds, do you say that I am?   -   Disciples
b. The response of the Disciples (Peter)   -   you are the Messiah
c. Jesus response -   I must be rejected & killed by elders, chief priests, teachers
d. Jesus demonstrates   -   Transfiguration (3), Moses & Elijah, God's voice

19. Jesus communicates death and rising to Disciples
(Matt 17:14-27; Mark 9:14-32; Luke 9:37-45)

a. The issue: What does rising from dead mean? -   crowd, teachers, disciples
b. The response of various groups   -   argument, conflict
c. Jesus responds   -   you unbelieving and perverse generation
                        -    delivered into hands of men, killed, third day rise
d. Jesus demonstrates   -   heals demon-possessed boy, coin in fish's mouth

20. Who is the greatest in the Kingdom of Heaven, who can & will follow
(Matt 18:1-35; Mark 9:33-50; Luke 9:46-62; John 7:1-8:11)

a. The issue: Who is the greatest?   -   Disciples, those who wish to follow
b. The response by men   -   Disciples arguing, Jewish leaders – 'kill him'
c. Jesus responds   -   don't cause stumbling, one sheep, sin in church
d. Jesus demonstrates   -   prevents woman from being stoned

Lessons 17-20

Jesus Shows that God's Gift of the Messiah Provides the Path to Heaven for Some: *Jesus teaches about the Kingdom of Heaven and how reaching it may be obstructed.*

17. The understanding & faith of the Disciples
18. Jesus recognized as Messiah, Savior by Disciples
19. Jesus communicates death and rising to Disciples
20. Who is the greatest in the Kingdom of Heaven, who can & will follow

This begins the second set of sixteen lessons (4 clusters of 4 lessons each).

In the first set of sixteen lessons God demonstrated that He offered the gift of his son to the world. Jesus demonstrated that the Father sent him, that Jesus has authority, that Jesus gives authority (e.g. to his disciples), that each person has authority over his or own heart to choose to believe, follow, and seek to share his love with others, and, that if one does so with faith, sins may be forgiven. Jesus makes clear that while he can heal all physical infirmity, deformity and disease, supply all physical needs of hunger and thirst, secure all natural phenomena, that it is the spiritual restoration and salvation that is above, behind and beyond the physical healings that is most important. He clearly locates the portal to forgiveness through faith in the heart ... the heart opens into the soul.

In the second set of sixteen lessons Jesus begins by showing that the heart of his 'little children' (disciples, believers) is defiled and demonized by those who encourage disbelief, specifically and especially the men who run religious and governmental institutions that emphasize the forceful 'rule of law' over the flow of the 'role and release of love'. The hearts of little children are filled with fear for their physical survival in the face of military might and control, and spiritual fear in the face of overburdening mental focus upon obeying complicated and overbearing rules promulgated by teachers of the law. Jesus turns to engage these men of status and power directly in these next lessons, giving them what they seek (to kill him), in order to display their lack of final authority, which is His.

Lesson 17: *Looking for Signs is Unbelief* (they cannot see or hear)

ISSUE. *Mathew 16: 1* The Pharisees and Sadducees came to Jesus and tested him by asking him to show them a sign from heaven.

DEMONSTRATION. *Mark 7: 32-35, Mark 8: 22-26* There some people brought to him a man who was deaf and could hardly talk, and they begged Jesus to place his hand on him. After he took him aside, away from the crowd, Jesus put his fingers into the man's ears. Then he spit and touched the man's tongue. He looked up to heaven and with a deep sigh said to him, *"Ephphatha!"* (which means "Be opened!"). At this, the man's ears were opened, his tongue was loosened and he began to speak plainly.

They came to Bethsaida, and some people brought a blind man and begged Jesus to touch him. He took the blind man by the hand and led him outside the village. When he had spit on the man's eyes and put his hands on him, Jesus asked, "Do you see anything?" He looked up and said, "I see people; they look like trees walking around." Once more Jesus put his hands on the man's eyes. Then his eyes were opened, his sight was restored, and he saw everything clearly. Jesus sent him home, saying, "Don't even go into the village."

Our Reflection: It is made simple and clear – open your eyes and ears to what is unseen and what you cannot hear, open the eyes of your heart, so that your soul might be restored to life.

Our Prayer: Lord, remove the obstacles to my seeing and hearing with my heart, that my soul might be restored to you, to me.

17. See & hear what you cannot, what is unseen and unsounded, *believe*	18.	19.	20.

Lesson 18: *Belief Blesses with the Kingdom of Heaven (listen to what is unseen)*

ISSUE. *Matthew 16: 13-20* When Jesus came to the region of Caesarea Philippi, he asked his disciples, "Who do people say the Son of Man is? "They replied, "Some say John the Baptist; others say Elijah; and still others, Jeremiah or one of the prophets." "But what about you?" he asked. "Who do you say I am?" Simon Peter answered, "You are the Messiah, the Son of the living God." Jesus replied, "Blessed are you, Simon son of Jonah, for this was not revealed to you by flesh and blood, but by my Father in heaven. And I tell you that you are Peter, and on this rock I will build my church, and the gates of Hades will not overcome it. I will give you the keys of the kingdom of heaven; whatever you bind on earth will be bound in heaven, and whatever you loose on earth will be loosed in heaven." Then he ordered his disciples not to tell anyone that he was the Messiah.

DEMONSTRATION. *Matthew 17: 1-8* After six days Jesus took with him Peter, James and John the brother of James, and led them up a high mountain by themselves. There he was transfigured before them. His face shone like the sun, and his clothes became as white as the light. Just then there appeared before them Moses and Elijah, talking with Jesus. Peter said to Jesus, "Lord, it is good for us to be here. If you wish, I will put up three shelters—one for you, one for Moses and one for Elijah." While he was still speaking, a bright cloud covered them, and a voice from the cloud said, "This is my Son, whom I love; with him I am well pleased. Listen to him!" When the disciples heard this, they fell facedown to the ground, terrified. But Jesus came and touched them. "Get up," he said. "Don't be afraid." When they looked up, they saw no one except Jesus.

Our Reflection: If we follow where Jesus leads, someday we may even hear the voice of God, as did Peter, James and John. Again, what we seek is so far beyond our common experience it may be terrifying, but our Lord comforts us so that we might not be afraid.

Our Prayer: *Lord, as the Father has directed, help to listen and hear ... with our hearts and our souls.*

17. *See & hear* what you cannot, what is unseen and unsounded, *believe*	18. *Follow* me and I will show you what cannot be found otherwise.	19.	20.

Lesson 19: *With Faith Nothing is Impossible (fear is what falls and fails, obstructing)*

ISSUE. *Matthew 17: 14-20* When they came to the crowd, a man approached Jesus and knelt before him. "Lord, have mercy on my son," he said. "He has seizures and is suffering greatly. He often falls into the fire or into the water. I brought him to your disciples, but they could not heal him." "You unbelieving and perverse generation," Jesus replied, "how long shall I stay with you? How long shall I put up with you? Bring the boy here to me." Jesus rebuked the demon, and it came out of the boy, and he was healed at that moment. Then the disciples came to Jesus in private and asked, "Why couldn't we drive it out?" He replied, "Because you have so little faith. Truly I tell you, if you have faith as small as a mustard seed, you can say to this mountain, 'Move from here to there,' and it will move. Nothing will be impossible for you."

DEMONSTRATION. *Matthew 17: 24-27* After Jesus and his disciples arrived in Capernaum, the collectors of the two-drachma temple tax came to Peter and asked, "Doesn't your teacher pay the temple tax?"
"Yes, he does," he replied. When Peter came into the house, Jesus was the first to speak. "What do you think, Simon?" he asked. "From whom do the kings of the earth collect duty and taxes—from their own children or from others?"
"From others," Peter answered.
"Then the children are exempt," Jesus said to him. "But so that we may not cause offense, go to the lake and throw out your line. Take the first fish you catch; open its mouth and you will find a four-drachma coin. Take it and give it to them for my tax and yours."

Our Reflection: Here is the shift in the ministry of Jesus, for the demon is unbelief and the antidote is faith, which even after all the demonstrations that Jesus performed, the disciples have difficulty finding in order to dispel unbelief. So here Jesus identifies the source of much of the unbelief in the people, the kings and rulers of the temple who take the money of families for food out of children's mouths, and, yet, he gives those of the temple what they ask for, in a way that demonstrates the Lord can supply all that is needed, if even to those who do not believe.

Our Prayer: Lord, the seed of my faith needs your life-giving water to grow, nourish us with such water turned to wine turned to blood turned to spirit and feed the fire in our soul for you.

17. *See & hear* what you cannot, what is unseen and unsounded, *believe*	18. *Follow* me and I will show you what cannot be found otherwise.	19. *Seek & share* faith (do not let the disbelief of others cause your unbelief)	20.

Lesson 20: *Humility and His Compassion Gives Life (others obstruct belief)*

ISSUE. *Matthew 18: 1-8* At that time the disciples came to Jesus and asked, "Who, then, is the greatest in the kingdom of heaven?" He called a little child to him, and placed the child among them. And he said: "Truly I tell you, unless you change and become like little children, you will never enter the kingdom of heaven. Therefore, whoever takes the lowly position of this child is the greatest in the kingdom of heaven. And whoever welcomes one such child in my name welcomes me. "If anyone causes one of these little ones—those who believe in me—to stumble, it would be better for them to have a large millstone hung around their neck and to be drowned in the depths of the sea. Woe to the world because of the things that cause people to stumble! Such things must come, but woe to the person through whom they come!

DEMONSTRATION. *John 8: 1-11 ... but Jesus went to the Mount of Olives.*
At dawn he appeared again in the temple courts, where all the people gathered around him, and he sat down to teach them. The teachers of the law and the Pharisees brought in a woman caught in adultery. They made her stand before the group and said to Jesus, "Teacher, this woman was caught in the act of adultery. In the Law Moses commanded us to stone such women. Now what do you say?" They were using this question as a trap, in order to have a basis for accusing him. But Jesus bent down and started to write on the ground with his finger. When they kept on questioning him, he straightened up and said to them, "Let any one of you who is without sin be the first to throw a stone at her." Again he stooped down and wrote on the ground. At this, those who heard began to go away one at a time, the older ones first, until only Jesus was left, with the woman still standing there. Jesus straightened up and asked her, "Woman, where are they? Has no one condemned you?"
"No one, sir," she said.
"Then neither do I condemn you," Jesus declared. "Go now and leave your life of sin."

Our Reflection: He calls his disciples and all those who believe 'his little ones' then identifies and warns those who would cause their innocent belief to falter, that they do not have the authority to judge such matters, for they are sinners as well. Neither does Jesus condemn, he saves through his compassionate forgiveness. He cautions his disciples (and their mother) not to seek status and position as do the priests and teachers of the law.

Our Prayer: *Lord, forgive us our trespasses as we forgive those who have trespassed against us, and hold and uplift us as the children we are, that we might laugh with joy in the hands and heart of your love.*

17. *See & hear* what you cannot, what is unseen and unsounded, *believe*	18. *Follow* me and I will show you what cannot be found otherwise.	19. *Seek & share* faith (do not let the disbelief of others cause your unbelief)	16. Sin no more, Be Forgiven, (Enable others to be forgiven & saved through *faith.*)

Lessons 21-24

Jesus Engages Institutions in Opposition to Him:
Jesus Teaches about Heaven and How it is Obstructed by Death

21. Dispute about testimony of Jesus   (John 8:12-9:12)

a. The issue: Your testimony is not valid, only your own witness - Pharisees

Who is Jesus?

b. The response of Jews   -   how can you free us ... we are children of Abraham, God

c. Jesus responds   -   if God your Father you would love me; devil is your father

d Jesus demonstrates   -   gives sight to man blind from birth ... I am the Light

22. Investigation of, questioning the works (healings) of Jesus
(John 9:13-10:41; Luke 11:1-13; Matt 6:9-13)

a. The issue: Man is not from God; heals blind man on Sabbath - Pharisees

b. The response of the Blind Man - if this man were not from God he could do
nothing

c. Jesus response -   if you claim you can see your guilt remains; love your God &
neighbor and you will live; sends 72 out to tell others

d. Jesus demonstrates   -   Martha don't worry, seek, listen and pray (Lord's Prayer)

23. Where power originates (Satan or God) in Jesus   (Luke 11:14-13:21)

a. The issue: is his power of Beelzebul?   -   some of the crowd

b. The response of various parties -   amazement; driven out by demon power

The response of a woman-blessed is the mother who gave you birth & nursed you

c. Jesus responds   -   woe to a wicked generation; see, repent, testify, be ready

d. Jesus demonstrates -   heals crippled woman on Sabbath; mustard seed, yeast

24. Institutional gatekeepers & hosts: The portal beyond death
(John 10:22-42; Luke 13:22-17:10; John 11:1-43)

a. The issue: Are you the Messiah or do you blaspheme?   -   Jewish opponents

b. The response by men   -   stone Jesus for blasphemy, invitees take places of
honor, Jerusalem kill prophets

c. Jesus responds   -   invite poor, be humble, hear, repent, serve, be faithful,
forgive & have faith

d. Jesus demonstrates   -   raises dead Lazarus; I am the Resurrection & the Life

Lessons 21-24

Jesus Engages Institutions in Opposition to Him:
Jesus teaches about Heaven and how it is obstructed by Death.

21. Dispute about testimony of Jesus ... SEE
22. Investigation of, questioning the works (healings) of Jesus ... HEAR
23. Where power originates (Satan or God) in Jesus ... SEEK
24. Institutional gatekeepers & hosts: The portal beyond death ... LIVE

Lesson 21: *SEE: Dispute about testimony of Jesus*

ISSUE. *John 8: 12-13* "I am the light of the world. Whoever follows me will never walk in darkness, but will have the light of life. "The Pharisees challenged him, "Here you are, appearing as your own witness; your testimony is not valid."

DEMONSTRATION. *John 9: 6-7* After saying this, he spit on the ground, made some mud with the saliva, and put it on the man's eyes. "Go," he told him, "wash in the Pool of Siloam" (this word means "Sent"). So the man went and washed, and came home seeing.

Our Reflection: Jesus makes clear that only those who believe in him, honor and love him will be able to see what only he has seen in the presence of the Father, being children of God. Disbelieving, dishonoring and denying who Jesus is – the Son of God – means those Jews cannot see, no matter how clear it is to be seen, making them the children of the evil one, the devil, who is a liar and has been from the beginning. Jesus has now clearly identified and defined the opposition to seeing and believing, while determining that we are all children.

Our Prayer: *Lord, as children we come to you, seeing by your light, gifted from the Father. Please help us to stay within the circle of your light, avoiding entering into the darkness where we would become lost.*

21. *See* what you cannot, what Jesus has seen, & *believe*	22.	23.	24.

Lesson 22: *HEAR*: Investigation of, questioning the works (healings) of Jesus

ISSUE. *John 9: 27-29* Then they asked him, "What did he do to you? How did he open your eyes?" He answered, "I have told you already and you did not listen. Why do you want to hear it again? Do you want to become his disciples too?"
Then they hurled insults at him and said, "You are this fellow's disciple! We are disciples of Moses! We know that God spoke to Moses, but as for this fellow, we don't even know where he comes from."

DEMONSTRATION. *Luke 10: 16; 38-42* "Whoever listens to you listens to me; whoever rejects you rejects me; but whoever rejects me rejects him who sent me." As Jesus and his disciples were on their way, he came to a village where a woman named Martha opened her home to him. She had a sister called Mary, who sat at the Lord's feet listening to what he said. But Martha was distracted by all the preparations that had to be made. She came to him and asked, "Lord, don't you care that my sister has left me to do the work by myself? Tell her to help me!" "Martha, Martha," the Lord answered, "you are worried and upset about many things, but few things are needed—or indeed only one. Mary has chosen what is better, and it will not be taken away from her."

Our Reflection: The Pharisees interrogate the blind man's parents and then the blind man (who can now see) himself. They listen but do not hear what the man and his parents have to confirm; that is, they do not believe that Jesus has done this and that he is the Son of God. Jesus states to the Pharisees that what he has heard from his Father (God) he tells to the world, that Jesus does nothing on his own but speaks just what the Father has taught him. Jesus tells the Pharisees that he is telling them what he has seen in the Father's presence and that they are only doing what they have heard from *their* father … not Abraham, but their father who is the devil, and therefore they are unable to hear what Jesus has to say, and, that, therefore they will die in their sins. Jesus tells the story of the Good Shepherd and his sheep – that the sheep know and listen to the shepherd's voice, he knows his sheep and his sheep know him, and that he is the gate through which they come in and out into good pastures. Jesus is not trying to prove anything to the Pharisees, they are already dead, he is just declaring what only he has seen and heard from the Father, what is unseen and unheard of by us, so that we may know His voice and his guidance.

Our Prayer: Lord, as children we follow you, follow the light and voicing of your word. What our eyes have not seen, but have yours, what our ears have not heard, but have yours, we open our the internal portal to our hearts so that your voice might reach and carry our souls to life.

21. *See* what you cannot, what Jesus has seen, & *believe*	22. *Hear & Follow* me and I will show you what cannot be found otherwise.	23.	24.

Lesson 23: *SEEK*

ISSUE. *Luke 11: 14-16* Jesus was driving out a demon that was mute. When the demon left, the man who had been mute spoke, and the crowd was amazed. But some of them said, "By Beelzebul, the prince of demons, he is driving out demons." Others tested him by asking for a sign from heaven.

DEMONSTRATION. *Luke 13: 10-13* On a Sabbath Jesus was teaching in one of the synagogues, and a woman was there who had been crippled by a spirit for eighteen years. She was bent over and could not straighten up at all. When Jesus saw her, he called her forward and said to her, "Woman, you are set free from your infirmity." Then he put his hands on her, and immediately she straightened up and praised God.

Our Reflection: Jesus indicates that he brings not peace but division, one who believes against one who disbelieves in the same family. He identifies the Pharisees and experts in the law as ones who are focused on the external rather than the internal, who neglect justice and the love of God, who are hypocrites, who persecute and execute God's prophets, and who conspire secretly within inner rooms to conceal their intents and actions. We understand that these men in powerful positions may motivate people to trample upon one another, yet when we come before them it is our work to testify to the truth as conveyed to us by Jesus, through the Holy Spirit.

Our Prayer: *Lord, help us to not be afraid, to not worry, about the cares of the world, but help us to voice the light of your Holy Spirit to those in positions of status and power, those who would use the law to have us trample one another, have us hurt one another or have us pretend to wash the outside of the cup rather than to cleanse and purify the inside.*

21. *See* what you cannot, what Jesus has seen, & *believe*	22. *Hear & Follow* me and I will show you what cannot be found otherwise.	23. *Seek & share* faith (do not let the disbelief of others cause your unbelief)	24.

Lesson 24: *LIVE*

ISSUE. *John10: 22-33* Then came the Festival of Dedication at Jerusalem. It was winter, and Jesus was in the temple courts walking in Solomon's Colonnade. The Jews who were there gathered around him, saying, "How long will you keep us in suspense? If you are the Messiah, tell us plainly." Jesus answered, "I did tell you, but you do not believe. The works I do in my Father's name testify about me, but you do not believe because you are not my sheep. My sheep listen to my voice; I know them, and they follow me. I give them eternal life, and they shall never perish; no one will snatch them out of my hand. My Father, who has given them to me, is greater than all; no one can snatch them out of my Father's hand. I and the Father are one." Again his Jewish opponents picked up stones to stone him, but Jesus said to them, "I have shown you many good works from the Father. For which of these do you stone me?" "We are not stoning you for any good work," they replied, "but for blasphemy, because you, a mere man, claim to be God."

DEMONSTRATION. *John 11: 38-44* Jesus, once more deeply moved, came to the tomb. It was a cave with a stone laid across the entrance. "Take away the stone," he said. "But, Lord," said Martha, the sister of the dead man, "by this time there is a bad odor, for he has been there four days. "Then Jesus said, "Did I not tell you that if you believe, you will see the glory of God?" So they took away the stone. Then Jesus looked up and said, "Father, I thank you that you have heard me. I knew that you always hear me, but I said this for the benefit of the people standing here, that they may believe that you sent me." When he had said this, Jesus called in a loud voice, "Lazarus, come out!" The dead man came out, his hands and feet wrapped with strips of linen, and a cloth around his face. Jesus said to them, "Take off the grave clothes and let him go."

Our Reflection: Jesus makes clear the sequence we must follow – lost, we must allow ourselves to be found so that we might see and believe; we must open and surrender, that is, open to be invited and then to come and hear, understand and follow; there is a path and portal where we do the work and know the entrance, entering we seek the kingdom of heaven; and, finally and most importantly we must love in order to live ... eternally.

Our Prayer: Lord, help to see and believe, hear and follow, share and eek, love and live.

21. *See* what you cannot, what Jesus has seen, *& believe*	22. *Hear & Follow* me and I will show you what cannot be found otherwise.	23. *Seek & share* faith (do not let the disbelief of others cause your unbelief)	24. Sin no more, Be Forgiven, (Be re-born into new, resurrected life through *faith*.)

Halfway through lessons 17-32 we have most of the little stories that Jesus offers to us, that provide us with a template, a detailed map, of what is involved in gaining the Kingdom of Heaven. Here are the 16 little stories arranged in the master four by four design, as well as our reflections ...

Sixteen Stories in Lessons 21-24

Lost :: *If Lost, Allow Yourself to be Found* :: **SEE**

24.7 one lost sheep (out of one hundred)
24.8 one lost coin (out of ten)
24.9 lost son (out of two)
22.2 Good Samaritan

Open & Surrender :: *Be Open to Be Invited and then Come* :: **HEAR**

24.5 building a tower (consider and prepare carefully the foundation)
24.6 king goes to war (consider the cost carefully and surrender what will be lost anyway)
24.4 man preparing a great banquet (invited, do not make excuse and refuse to come)
24.3 invited to wedding feast taking place of honor (be humble, invite poor)

The Path and Portal :: *Do the Work, Know the Entrance, Enter the Door Humbly* ::
SEEK

22.1 Good shepherd and the gate (follow and enter through me)
24.1 enter through the narrow door (make every effort to enter)
23.5 Servants waiting and watching (ready to open door, do his work meanwhile)
24.13 servant plowing field comes in to eat (we are unworthy, only doing our duty)

Love :: *Love with all your Heart, with all your Soul, all your Strength, all your mind* ::
LIVE

23.1 lamp of the body (eyes lamp of body and light inside and out, avoid darkness)
24.10 rich man, manager and debtors (trustworthy serve God not money)
23.2 Rich fool (greed is storing up what will perish)
24.11 rich man, beggar named Lazarus, Abraham (share good things with unfortunate)

[lesson number.number of stories in that lesson] ... 24.11 = the eleventh story in Lesson Twenty-four]

Seeing and Believing That One is Lost *(repent)*

This first cluster of four little stories in the second set of lessons is about being lost. The first story starts with a shepherd valuing one lost sheep above the ninety-nine who are safe. The one sheep might continue to wander in confusion and will not be able to find its way home itself; it can only be saved if it realizes it is lost and cries out to be found. The second story involves a woman who has ten silver coins and knows the high value of each one, but somehow loses one of these precious coins. Where one sheep might be seen as insignificant in relation to 99, there is no question that a single silver coin is of great value and must be found. There is rejoicing as both the shepherd and the woman persist until they bring home what is precious. The third story significantly extends the first two by beginning to suggest that the nature of the valuing is of the heart – a young son left the loving context of his father to go taste worldly things, realized his folly and returned, repentant. The older, righteous son who had faithfully served his father was angry and indignant, not understanding that the father's love for his lost son, the son who was dead and who was now alive, was the reason for the celebration. The older son did not understand that it was not his own work that was most important, but his father's love for both of his sons that was primary. If you can see, you can be found when you are lost. If you can hear the tender caring in the love that would be gifted you regardless of your own efforts, such love might be shared as a shining light for others to see, hear and be comforted by. Such experience can then be welcomed into their own hearts, as a beacon for the love they too may seek, find, purchase, store and share, ... as in the case of the poor man who had been stripped, robbed, beaten and then rescued, not by a priest or teacher, by but a passing good stranger (Samaritan).

Hearing and Understanding the Invitation *(surrender)*

In the second cluster of four little stories, what is of value has been identified and spread into additional forms – the love of the lord of a castle to keep his people safe, love of a king for his people, the generosity of one giving a banquet to his guests, and the honoring of guests by the banquet giver – and the cost that may accrue to such love and generosity to the giver and the danger to those who are invited if they do not attend. In the first story a man need estimate the cost of a tower before he builds it to know if he can finish it ... could you give everything, even your life to complete the job? The second story describes a much larger example in the situation of king needing to assess a very large and powerful enemy and the cost it would be to his people if he went to war. Being the king of your own heart do you really want to be against what may be the most powerful authority you will ever know, and, paradoxically, suing for peace with this authority means paying a hefty cost of giving up all you own and have? The third story characterizes this authority not as an opposing king, but as the host of a great banquet who is inviting you to the feast of everlasting life ... do you really want to make excuses and not attend; do you realize what you are turning down!? And the fourth story in this cluster completes the sequence by telling of being invited to a wedding feast and whether it is wise, as you have been invited, to think that you might give yourself a position of honor rather than humbly take a low enough position at the table (if that is possible), so that at the very least you will not be moved lower, but might even be exalted to a higher place of honor. Thus, we have the cost of the life we build, the cost of the larger life we choose to live, seeing, hearing and surrendering to the nature of the invitation that has been made to us, and being appropriately humble to the undeserved place we may have at the table of celebration.

Find and Enter the Portal (seek)

In the third cluster of four little stories, the focus shifts to the path home to the kingdom of heaven, that place which holds the treasure that has been sought by each person, family household, and community. In the first little story we are told that there is a voice that guides into a safe enclosure and out into green pastures, and that the gateway through which such safe passage can only be made is only located with the help of the voice of the good shepherd (referring to the fact that only the Son has seen and heard the Father, and that the Son's voice is also the voice of the Father). The second story suggests that the door is narrow through which such passage is made into such a safe haven and made clear that the door into this home will be closed by the owner and whomever is left outside will not gain passage through once it is closed. This portal of the heart is described from the inside, in the third little story about servants dressed and ready for the master of their hearts coming home from a wedding banquet. The servants are cautioned to be watchful and ready, to bar the door to their heart from any thief entering, but ready to open it for their master who will then serve them at the table while they recline. Indeed, the servants are also cautioned that their hearts must be taking care of the possessions of the master and doing his will or they will be cut to pieces and placed with the unbelievers. And in the final little story that completes this sequence and progression, we are told that if the hearts of the servants have been out plowing and planting the fields or gathering and safeguarding the sheep, when they finally come into the heart of the home of their master, should humbly express that they have done their duty and only seek to continue to serve their master therein. So have we learned that there is a portal into the kingdom of heaven, that is narrow and that it will be closed some day. The portal to our souls is located in our hearts, which must be waiting and watching, ready and serving the love of our master that is here and that is coming.

Live Through Your Heart Into Your Soul (love)

In the fourth and final cluster of four little stories, the battle between light and darkness in our hearts, the challenge of finding and holding on to the treasure that is the seed (the word) and the kingdom of heaven, and the precious pursuit of our souls along the passage and through portal into the love of the Son and the Father, is truly enjoined and completed. In the first little story the light in your heart must not be tainted with any darkness, so that you are not darkness, and the light of God's love that shines on and into your heart shines out of it as well. In the second little story we find that in order to manage a rich man's possessions a manager must do so shrewdly and that while children of the light (of the love of God) should not place wealth above God, they might give wealth away in order to spread generosity (a form of the light) and secure a place in the dwelling of eternity. In the third little story we are again cautioned against greed as a rich man stores up his harvest for himself but will not enjoy his worldly treasure and wealth if he dies not having given richly toward God or others. In the fourth story, the outcome is made clear as a rich man living in luxury and a beggar (Lazarus) both die, the poor man going into the kingdom of heaven and the rich man into Hades. Regretfully, but too late, the rich man seeks a tiny drop of water in the midst of the flames or at least a warning being given to his living brothers, but there is no portal or path between the two realms, only a great impassable chasm, so the rich man remains in his torment-without-ceasing. These stories make clear that seeking the light, accumulating it, shining and sharing it outwards, lighting the way of others leads to that which is imperishable, is much to be preferred to accumulating the darkness of *getting* that which is of least value and that which perishes.

Please note the primary actors in the previous lessons 17-24 and their associated little stories. Imagine if this list were composed of the equivalent participants in each category today, within which one you might be included:

Elements and Actors

Divine Authority
Host, master
Servant, manager
Abraham, Moses and Prophets, Isaac & Jacob

Those with Status, Power and Position

Jerusalem, Temple	*stone prophets, kill those sent*
Jewish opponents	*do not believe, try to seize, kill*
Pharisees, Teachers/experts of the law	*exalt themselves, invite friends to*
Herod, Sanhedrin	*be repaid*
Rich man	*live in luxury, serve money*

Followers and Family
Older brother, five brothers, two sisters (Mary and Martha), brother (Lazarus)
Father, mother, wife, children, brother, sisters
Beggar Lazarus
Disciples

Souls
Tax collectors, sinners
Lost coin, lost sheep, lost son
Poor, crippled, lame, blind , guests, debtors

Lessons 25-28

Jesus Engages Belief and Unbelief:
Jesus Predicts His Death

25. Shall Jesus die for the Jewish nation?   (John 11:43-54; Luke 17:11-19)

a. The issue: What should be done about, with Jesus?   -   Sanhedrin
b. The response of high priest Caiaphas   -   Jesus should die for the Jewish nation
c. Jesus responds   -   stayed with disciples near wilderness
d Jesus demonstrates   -   heals ten men with leprosy & sends them to the priests

26. What is the coming of the kingdom of God?   (Luke 17:20-18:43; Matt 19:1-20:34; Mark 10; 1-52)

a. The issue: When will the kingdom of God come; where?   -   Pharisees; disciples
b. The response of the people; Pharisees   -   When will justice come? What to do to inherit eternal life? Is divorce lawful?
c. Jesus response   -   give everything away; follow me; the last shall be first
d. Jesus demonstrates   -   two blind beggars receive their sight

27. Who and what is the king of the Jews?
    (Luke 19:1-48; John 11:55-12:1, 9-19, 2:13-22; Matt 21:1-19; Mark 11:1-18)

a. The issue: Dining with sinners   -   the people
b. The response of the people   -   associating with sinners is wrong
c. Jesus responds   -   who has more will be given, who has nothing all taken
d. Jesus demonstrates -   rides in on donkey; heals lame & blind; curses fig tree; clears temple

28. How does death glorify?   (John 12:20-50; Matt:21:20-22; Mark 11:19-25)

a. The issue: Greeks would like to see Jesus   -   Gentiles
b. The response by men   -   law says the Messiah will remain forever; blinded their eyes, hardened their hearts
c. Jesus responds   -   a seed dies to produce many seeds; hear my words & keep them; pray, ask & have fait
d. Jesus demonstrates   -   fig tree withered

Lesson 25: *SEE WHAT IS UNSEEN*

ISSUE. *John 11: 45-53* Therefore many of the Jews who had come to visit Mary, and had seen what Jesus did, believed in him. But some of them went to the Pharisees and told them what Jesus had done. Then the chief priests and the Pharisees called a meeting of the Sanhedrin. "What are we accomplishing?" they asked. "Here is this man performing many signs. If we let him go on like this, everyone will believe in him, and then the Romans will come and take away both our temple and our nation." Then one of them, named Caiaphas, who was high priest that year, spoke up, "You know nothing at all! You do not realize that it is better for you that one man die for the people than that the whole nation perish." He did not say this on his own, but as high priest that year he prophesied that Jesus would die for the Jewish nation, and not only for that nation but also for the scattered children of God, to bring them together and make them one. So from that day on they plotted to take his life.

DEMONSTRATION. *Luke 17: 11-19* Now on his way to Jerusalem, Jesus traveled along the border between Samaria and Galilee. As he was going into a village, ten men who had leprosy met him. They stood at a distance and called out in a loud voice, "Jesus, Master, have pity on us!" When he saw them, he said, "Go, show yourselves to the priests." And as they went, they were cleansed. One of them, when he saw he was healed, came back, praising God in a loud voice. He threw himself at Jesus' feet and thanked him—and he was a Samaritan. Jesus asked, "Were not all ten cleansed? Where are the other nine? Has no one returned to give praise to God except this foreigner?" Then he said to him, "Rise and go; your faith has made you well."

Our Reflection: Jesus, his disciples and followers are on their way to Jerusalem, toward the center of the darkness hidden within institutional blindness and the wielding of political and military power of the times, to confront the rule of law with the penetrating power of love. These powers try to twist the teachings of Jesus that create a path for the salvation of souls ... into a warped justification 'so that the Jewish Nation will not perish', meaning they will kill him to insure the continuation of their own status, position and power. This pretention is revealed when Jesus cleanses ten lepers and sends them to the priests, showing the priests what they must do – cleanse themselves – and praise God that His Son has come to cleanse the world of such sin, as savior and salvation. Only one of the ten returns to Jesus in thanksgiving and praise, indicating how many miss this direction.

Our Prayer: Lord, help to see and believe the true path, created by your hands and feet and heart, forsaking the pretension of position and power, rather humbly praising God that you might cleanse our souls, rinsing and releasing our sins in the sacrifice of your forgiveness.

25. *See & believe* that each might be cleansed of the worldly debris of sin	26.	27.	28.

Lesson 26: *HEAR WHAT YOU CANNOT SEE*

ISSUE. *Luke 17: 20-22* Once, on being asked by the Pharisees when the kingdom of God would come, Jesus replied, "The coming of the kingdom of God is not something that can be observed, nor will people say, 'Here it is,' or 'There it is,' because the kingdom of God is in your midst." Then he said to his disciples, "The time is coming when you will long to see one of the days of the Son of Man, but you will not see it.

DEMONSTRATION. *Matthew 20: 29-34; Mark 10: 52; Luke 18: 42-43* As Jesus and his disciples were leaving Jericho, a large crowd followed him. Two blind men were sitting by the roadside, and when they heard that Jesus was going by, they shouted, "Lord, Son of David, have mercy on us!" The crowd rebuked them and told them to be quiet, but they shouted all the louder, "Lord, Son of David, have mercy on us!" Jesus stopped and called them. "What do you want me to do for you?" he asked. "Lord," they answered, "we want our sight." Jesus had compassion on them and touched their eyes. Immediately they received their sight and followed him. (Jesus said to him, "Receive your sight; your faith has healed you." Immediately he received his sight and followed Jesus, praising God. When all the people saw it, they also praised God.)

Our Reflection: Jesus makes clear what to **beseech** the Father for: In the story of the widow and the judge it is *justice*; in the story of the Pharisee and tax collector praying it is not for recognition of self-determined righteousness, but for *mercy*; in the story of the workers hired to work in the vineyard it is not for self-determined reward, but for generous God-determined *grace and charity*. What we ask for should not be positions of honor as the mother of James and John asked for her sons, but we should come with the *innocence* of children into the arms of our Lord. Once again, at the end of this lesson disciples and followers obstruct the little ones – children and blind beggars – who are crying out to hear the words of and be with the Jesus. Yet, Jesus asked his followers <u>not</u> to rebuke those who sought comfort, healing, or to get close enough to hear and follow his voice, to be caught by its wondrously sacred word. What we try to save for ourselves will be lost and what we give of our life to others will continue, as Jesus predicts the giving of his life for ours is about to happen in Jerusalem.

Our Prayer: Lord, help to see and believe what cannot be seen, hear and follow that voice that is yours that is within us, all the while not getting in the way of others who are striving to get close to you, as well.

25. *See & believe* that each might be cleansed of the worldly debris of sin.	26. *Hear & Follow* me and I will show and tell you what cannot be found otherwise.	27.	28.

Lesson 27: *SEEK WHAT YOU CANNOT SEE OR HEAR*

ISSUE. *Luke 19: 1-7* Jesus entered Jericho and was passing through. A man was there by the name of Zacchaeus; he was a chief tax collector and was wealthy. He wanted to see who Jesus was, but because he was short he could not see over the crowd. So he ran ahead and climbed a sycamore-fig tree to see him, since Jesus was coming that way. When Jesus reached the spot, he looked up and said to him, "Zacchaeus, come down immediately. I must stay at your house today." So he came down at once and welcomed him gladly. All the people saw this and began to mutter, "He has gone to be the guest of a sinner."

DEMONSTRATION. *Mark 11: 15-18* On reaching Jerusalem, Jesus entered the temple courts and began driving out those who were buying and selling there. He overturned the tables of the money changers and the benches of those selling doves, and would not allow anyone to carry merchandise through the temple courts. And as he taught them, he said, "Is it not written: 'My house will be called a house of prayer for all nations'? But you have made it 'a den of robbers.'" The chief priests and the teachers of the law heard this and began looking for a way to kill him, for they feared him, because the whole crowd was amazed at his teaching.

Our Reflection: Jesus descries and clears out the enterprises of the worldly temple, while responding positively to the zeal of one who seeks Him, even though the seeker is obstructed by his shortness and the crowds. The pairing in this lesson of the fig tree which does not produce fruit that Jesus causes to whither and die, with the sycamore-fig tree that Zacchaeus climbs from which Jesus 'picks' him, makes it quite clear what we are to persistently seek – souls from and for the tree of life. Jesus further details how to bear and produce fruit in his little story of the servants who were given ten minas (golden love) ... each of us must nurture and produce more fruit than we have been given from the seeds (Holy Word and Spirit) that Jesus gave us to, plant, grow and harvest ... to sow and reap love faithfully. Jesus rides into Jerusalem as the Prince of Peace and final authority and arbiter of this harvest of love as who will enter the kingdom of heaven as he enters Jerusalem triumphant.

Our Prayer: Lord, help us to see and believe what is unseen but in the midst of us, to hear and follow the path you have taken of giving all so that others might live, and to seek your Word, Spirit and Presence, sharing the gifts with others as you have shared them with us.

25. *See & believe* that each might be cleansed of the worldly debris of sin.	26. *Hear & Follow* me and I will show and tell you what cannot be found otherwise.	27. *Seek & share* faith (do not let fear or other conditions cause unfruitfulness).	28.

Lesson 28: *LIVE IN THE LIGHT OR DIE IN THE DARKNESS*

ISSUE. *John 12: 20-36* Now there were some Greeks among those who went up to worship at the festival. They came to Philip, who was from Bethsaida in Galilee, with a request. "Sir," they said, "we would like to see Jesus." Philip went to tell Andrew; Andrew and Philip in turn told Jesus. Jesus replied, "The hour has come for the Son of Man to be glorified. Very truly I tell you, unless a kernel of wheat falls to the ground and dies, it remains only a single seed. But if it dies, it produces many seeds. Anyone who loves their life will lose it, while anyone who hates their life in this world will keep it for eternal life. Whoever serves me must follow me; and where I am, my servant also will be. My Father will honor the one who serves me." Now my soul is troubled, and what shall I say? 'Father, save me from this hour'? No, it was for this very reason I came to this hour. Father, glorify your name!" Then a voice came from heaven, "I have glorified it, and will glorify it again." The crowd that was there and heard it said it had thundered; others said an angel had spoken to him. Jesus said, "This voice was for your benefit, not mine. Now is the time for judgment on this world; now the prince of this world will be driven out. And I, when I am lifted up from the earth, will draw all people to myself." He said this to show the kind of death he was going to die. The crowd spoke up, "We have heard from the Law that the Messiah will remain forever, so how can you say, 'The Son of Man must be lifted up'? Who is this 'Son of Man'?" Then Jesus told them, "You are going to have the light just a little while longer. Walk while you have the light, before darkness overtakes you. Whoever walks in the dark does not know where they are going. Believe in the light while you have the light, so that you may become children of light." When he had finished speaking, Jesus left and hid himself from them. Even after Jesus had performed so many signs in their presence, they still would not believe in him.

DEMONSTRATION. *Mark 11: 12-14; 20-36* The next day as they were leaving Bethany, Jesus was hungry. Seeing in the distance a fig tree in leaf, he went to find out if it had any fruit. When he reached it, he found nothing but leaves, because it was not the season for figs. Then he said to the tree, "May no one ever eat fruit from you again." And his disciples heard him say it. When evening came, Jesus and his disciples went out of the city.... In the morning, as they went along, they saw the fig tree withered from the roots. Peter remembered and said to Jesus, "Rabbi, look! The fig tree you cursed has withered!" "Have faith in God," Jesus answered. "Truly I tell you, if anyone says to this mountain, 'Go, throw yourself into the sea,' and <u>does not doubt in their heart</u> but believes that what they say will happen, it will be done for them. Therefore I tell you, whatever you ask for in prayer, believe that you have received it, and it will be yours. And when you stand praying, if you hold anything against anyone, forgive them, so that your Father in heaven may forgive you your sins."

Our Reflection: In this lesson John (*John 12: 37-50*) testifies it most clearly – Even after Jesus performs so many signs in their presence, they still would not believe in him. This fulfills the word of Isaiah that some believe the revealed message, but many could not believe because their eyes were blinded, their <u>hearts</u>

hardened, so they can neither see with their eyes, nor understand with their hearts, nor turn—so that Jesus would heal them.

Yet many among the leaders believed in him. But because of the Pharisees they would not openly acknowledge their faith for fear they would be put out of the synagogue; for they loved human praise more than praise from God. Jesus cried out, "Whoever believes in me does not believe in me only, but in the one who sent me. The one who looks at me is seeing the one who sent me. I have come into the world as a light, so that no one who believes in me should stay in darkness. If anyone hears my words but does not keep them, I do not judge that person. For I did not come to judge the world, but to save the world. There is a judge for the one who rejects me and does not accept my words; the very words I have spoken will condemn them at the last day. For I did not speak on my own, but the Father who sent me commanded me to say all that I have spoken. I know that his command leads to eternal life. So whatever I say is just what the Father has told me to say."

It is very clear to us in these passages that it is *'seeing with the heart'* that allows entry into the portal that is the soul. Into and through the softened and opened heart is poured the Lord's love, into the soul, and it is the presence of this Holy Love and Spirit dwelling in the soul that the mind recognizes and believes.

Our Prayer: *Lord, help to open our hearts so that your love may be poured in, so that we might see and believe, hear and follow, share and seek, love in our turn and live ... that is, help us to become children of light.*

25. *See & believe* that each might be cleansed of the worldly debris of sin.	26. *Hear & Follow* me and I will show and tell you what cannot be found otherwise.	27. *Seek & share* faith (do not let fear or other conditions cause unfruitfulness).	24. Be Forgiven, Praise God (Be re-born into new, resurrected life through *faith.*)

Lessons 29-32

Jesus Reveals the Nature of Power:
The Judgment and Killing of Jesus by Human Authority

29. Who has authority?   (Matt 21:23-23:39; Mark 11:27-12:40; Luke 20:1-42)

a. The issue: By what authority are you doing these things? - chief priests & elders
b. The response of priests & elders - we do not know who authorized John's baptism
c. Jesus responds   -   tax collectors & prostitutes believed but you did not;
                                        kingdom of God taken away; give back to Caesar
d Jesus demonstrates   -   poor widow giving all she had to live on

30. What is appropriate response to institutional power?
          (Matt 24:1-26:13; Mark 13:1-14:9; Luke 21:5-22:2, 7:36-50; John 12:2-8)

a. The issue: When is sign of coming & end of age?   -   Disciples
b. The response of the people   -   many will be deceived; love of most will
                                                                              grow cold
c. Jesus response - stand firm; watch for the coming on the clouds of heaven; day
                                                                      & hour unknown
d. Jesus demonstrates   -   anointed by a sinful woman with oil

31. Comfort, betrayal and denial ... the Holy Spirit?
          (Matt 26:14-62;Mark 14:10-60; Luke 22:3-54; John 13:1-18:14)

a. The issue: Who will deliver Jesus?   -   Chief Priest; Judas
b. The response of the disciples   -   shock & denial
c. Jesus responds   -   you will betray me; you will deny me
                                    -     last supper; work of Holy Spirit, Gethsemane
d. Jesus demonstrates   -   arrest

32. Judgment and death?
     (Matt 26:57-27:59; Mark 14:53-15:41; Luke 22:54-23:49; John18:15-19:39)

a. The issue: How to accuse, jusdge Jesus?   -   Sanhedrin,; Pilate; Herod
b. The response by the priests   -   blasphemy
c. Jesus responds   -   no response, so you have said, I am

d. Jesus demonstrates   -   allow himself to be sentenced & crucified

Lesson 29: *SEE WHAT IS UNSEEN*

ISSUE. *Matthew 21: 23-27* Jesus entered the temple courts, and, while he was teaching, the chief priests and the elders of the people came to him. "By what authority are you doing these things?" they asked. "And who gave you this authority?" Jesus replied, "I will also ask you one question. If you answer me, I will tell you by what authority I am doing these things. John's baptism—where did it come from? Was it from heaven, or of human origin?" They discussed it among themselves and said, "If we say, 'From heaven,' he will ask, 'Then why didn't you believe him?' But if we say, 'Of human origin'—we are afraid of the people, for they all hold that John was a prophet." So they answered Jesus, "We don't know."
Then he said, "Neither will I tell you by what authority I am doing these things."

DEMONSTRATION. *Mark 12: 41-44* Jesus sat down opposite the place where the offerings were put and watched the crowd putting their money into the temple treasury. Many rich people threw in large amounts. But a poor widow came and put in two very small copper coins, worth only a few cents. Calling his disciples to him, Jesus said, "Truly I tell you, this poor widow has put more into the treasury than all the others. They all gave out of their wealth; but she, out of her poverty, put in everything—all she had to live on."

Our Reflection: If it is so very hard for a rich man to pass through the narrow portal into the kingdom of heaven, how much harder must it be for one bestowed gifts of mind that lead into positions of respect, admiration, status and power on earth. For Jesus told us to call no one rabbi, father or instructor. The greatest will be the humble servant, while those who are exalted (and who exalt themselves) will be humbled. Jesus called the teachers of the law and the Pharisees blind hypocrites, full of wicked greed and self-indulgence, unclean on the inside while appearing beautiful on the outside. He descried the neglect of justice, mercy and faithfulness. There are little stories in this lesson: The two sons –one who said he would not work but did and one who said he would but did not ; the vineyard owner renting to farmers who kept the harvest for themselves, abusing and killing the owners servants and son; and the king who prepared a wedding banquet, whose invited guest ignored, mistreated and killed the servants sent to tell them it was ready and to come. These were those who did not see and recognize the importance of what was being given, who did not listen and realize the precious relationship being offered, who did not heed and welcome the invitation, denying the true relations being represented between king/master/owner and subject/servant. They did not realize that loving God and their fellow man is always paramount.

Our Prayer: Lord, help to see and believe, hear and follow, seek and share, your love.

29. *See & believe* (for if you do not there is only desolation and despair in the darkness)	30.	31.	32.

Lesson 30: *HEAR WHAT YOU CANNOT SEE*

ISSUE. *Mark 13: 1-4* As Jesus was leaving the temple, one of his disciples said to him, "Look, Teacher! What massive stones! What magnificent buildings!"
"Do you see all these great buildings?" replied Jesus. "Not one stone here will be left on another; every one will be thrown down." As Jesus was sitting on the Mount of Olives opposite the temple, Peter, James, John and Andrew asked him privately, "Tell us, when will these things happen? And what will be the sign that they are all about to be fulfilled?"

DEMONSTRATION. *Matthew 26: 6-13;Luke 7* While Jesus was in Bethany in the home of Simon the Leper, a woman came to him with an alabaster jar of very expensive perfume, which she poured on his head as he was reclining at the table. When the disciples saw this, they were indignant. "Why this waste?" they asked. "This perfume could have been sold at a high price and the money given to the poor." Aware of this, Jesus said to them, "Why are you bothering this woman? She has done a beautiful thing to me. The poor you will always have with you,[a] but you will not always have me. When she poured this perfume on my body, she did it to prepare me for burial. Truly I tell you, wherever this gospel is preached throughout the world, what she has done will also be told, in memory of her." ...
 Therefore, I tell you, her many sins have been forgiven—as her great love has shown. But whoever has been forgiven little loves little." Then Jesus said to her, "Your sins are forgiven." The other guests began to say among themselves, "Who is this who even forgives sins?" Jesus said to the woman, "Your faith has saved you; go in peace."

Our Reflection: Jesus offers the final four little stories in the Gospels that outline the fundamental way to enter the kingdom of heaven and have the kingdom heaven enter you. The story of the man going on a journey entrusting his wealth to servants speaks of increasing the abundance the Lord has abundantly given us. The story of the wise and foolish virgins waiting for the bridegroom of the kingdom of heaven with lamps, speaks of always being prepared to offer that abundance in the form of light ... lighting the way for your self, for others, for the One to come, ... lighting the way to the door through which the blessed may pass. The sharing of this abundance and light is specified in the story of the Son of Man separating souls into sheep and goats - those that feed bread to the hungry, wet the thirsty with water and wine, and comfort the unclothed, ill and imprisoned with the warm fire and light of the Spirit. The final little story of two people owing different amounts to a moneylender embraces that greater forgiveness begets greater love. The lesson culminates in the demonstration of Mary's anointing Jesus with her love before his impending death and burial and his forgiving her sins based upon her loving faith and embracing her with his peace.

Our Prayer: Lord, help to see and believe, hear and follow, seek and share, your love.

29. *See & believe* (for if you do not there is only desolation and despair in the darkness)	30. *Hear & Follow* (the path of 'abundance given' lights the way, if offered to others)	31.	32.

Lesson 31: *SEEK & SHARE WHAT YOU CANNOT SEE OR HEAR*

ISSUE. *Mathew 26: 14-16* Then one of the Twelve—the one called Judas Iscariot—went to the chief priests and asked, "What are you willing to give me if I deliver him over to you?" So they counted out for him thirty pieces of silver. From then on Judas watched for an opportunity to hand him over.

DEMONSTRATION. *John 18: 1-14* When he had finished praying, Jesus left with his disciples and crossed the Kidron Valley. On the other side there was a garden, and he and his disciples went into it. Now Judas, who betrayed him, knew the place, because Jesus had often met there with his disciples. So Judas came to the garden, guiding a detachment of soldiers and some officials from the chief priests and the Pharisees. They were carrying torches, lanterns and weapons. Jesus, knowing all that was going to happen to him, went out and asked them, "Who is it you want?" "Jesus of Nazareth," they replied. "I am he," Jesus said. (And Judas the traitor was standing there with them.) When Jesus said, "I am he," they drew back and fell to the ground. Again he asked them, "Who is it you want?" "Jesus of Nazareth," they said. Jesus answered, "I told you that I am he. If you are looking for me, then let these men go." This happened so that the words he had spoken would be fulfilled: "I have not lost one of those you gave me." Then Simon Peter, who had a sword, drew it and struck the high priest's servant, cutting off his right ear. (The servant's name was Malchus.) Jesus commanded Peter, "Put your sword away! Shall I not drink the cup the Father has given me?" Then the detachment of soldiers with its commander and the Jewish officials arrested Jesus. They bound him and brought him first to Annas, who was the father-in-law of Caiaphas, the high priest that year. Caiaphas was the one who had advised the Jewish leaders that it would be good if one man died for the people.

Our Reflection: In this lesson, Jesus re-enacts the four-part design we have been studying thus far, at the deepest level. He

1) finds a physical place (an upper room) for their last supper together,
2) cleanses them (washes their feet),
3) feeds them with bread (his body), wine (his blood), and his Holy Spirit and then
4) comforts them with the certainty that where he is going he and the Father have a place for them and that they know the way.

Then Jesus describes
1) how he is the way to the Father,
2) promises them the advocate of the Holy Spirit and how the Holy Spirit will work with them to glorify the Father and Son,
3) tells them that the Father is the Gardener, he the vine and the disciples the branches and fruit who will be hated by the world because they are not of this world; and then
4) comforts them once again in terms of how their grief will be turned to joy as a mother endures her pain to rejoice at newborn life.

Finally, Jesus prays in four parts - first to glorify the Father, second to protect his disciples from the evil one, third for the believers to become one as the Father and the Son are one, and finally, for comfort from the Father as Jesus allows his arrest and death at the hands of the authorities ... while his disciples respectively sleep, deny, flee and abandon him.

This four-part pattern reiterates the primary sacred questions:

Do you recognize the reality that you are a child of God, the Father and Creator, and that he has chosen you to be children of Light and has a place for you?

Do you realize a relationship with God the Son and Savior, that he might wash and cleanse you of your sins in the light of his perfect love, forgive you and show you the way, through him, to the kingdom of Heaven, through the portal of love, penetrating death, to the place that the Father and Son have created for you?

Do you represent the relations of this Truth, through the accompaniment and advocacy of God the Holy Spirit, placed into each believer's heart to voice the Word (works and witness) to others so that they might become one with all believers, one with the Son and Father who sent him, abundantly and richly love-bearing fruits of other souls saved?

And, finally, do you re-compose yourself in prayers of glorification and praise, of gratitude and grace, of love shared into a life fulfilling faith, and rest in the most humble silence that allows the sacred peace of God to descend into our soul, as we are one in the kingdom and the power and the glory, forever and ever.

Our Prayer: *Lord, help us to see and believe in the place you have created and preserved for us called the kingdom of heaven, help us to hear and follow the power of love to restore our hearts, help us to seek and share the truth of faithful service as a way to conserve our souls for you and your glory, and sanctify the consecration of your love in our lives and deaths, as well, for all eternity.*

29. *See & believe* (for if you do not there is only desolation and despair in the darkness)	30. *Hear & Follow* (the path of 'abundant love given' lights the way, if offered to others)	31. *Seek & Share* (feed faith in forgiveness through the truth of expressed mercy, charity and love)	32.

Lesson 32: *LIVE IN THE LIGHT OR DIE IN THE DARKNESS*

ISSUE. *Mathew 26: 57-68* Those who had arrested Jesus took him to Caiaphas the high priest, where the teachers of the law and the elders had assembled. But Peter followed him at a distance, right up to the courtyard of the high priest. He entered and sat down with the guards to see the outcome. The chief priests and the whole Sanhedrin were looking for false evidence against Jesus so that they could put him to death. But they did not find any, though many false witnesses came forward. Finally two came forward and declared, "This fellow said, 'I am able to destroy the temple of God and rebuild it in three days.'" Then the high priest stood up and said to Jesus, "Are you not going to answer? What is this testimony that these men are bringing against you?" But Jesus remained silent. The high priest said to him, "I charge you under oath by the living God: Tell us if you are the Messiah, the Son of God." "You have said so," Jesus replied. "But I say to all of you: From now on you will see the Son of Man sitting at the right hand of the Mighty One and coming on the clouds of heaven." Then the high priest tore his clothes and said, "He has spoken blasphemy! Why do we need any more witnesses? Look, now you have heard the blasphemy. What do you think?" "He is worthy of death," they answered. Then they spit in his face and struck him with their fists. Others slapped him and said, "Prophesy to us, Messiah. Who hit you?"

DEMONSTRATION. *Mark 15: 33-41* At noon, darkness came over the whole land until three in the afternoon. And at three in the afternoon Jesus cried out in a loud voice, *"Eloi, Eloi, lema sabachthani?"* (which means "My God, my God, why have you forsaken me?"). When some of those standing near heard this, they said, "Listen, he's calling Elijah." Someone ran, filled a sponge with wine vinegar, put it on a staff, and offered it to Jesus to drink. "Now leave him alone. Let's see if Elijah comes to take him down," he said. With a loud cry, Jesus breathed his last. The curtain of the temple was torn in two from top to bottom. And when the centurion, who stood there in front of Jesus, saw how he died, he said, "Surely this man was the Son of God!" Some women were watching from a distance. Among them were Mary Magdalene, Mary the mother of James the younger and of Joseph, and Salome. In Galilee these women had followed him and cared for his needs. Many other women who had come up with him to Jerusalem were also there.

Our Reflection: Placed in the hands of the earthly authorities, Jesus answers their questions "If I tell, you will not believe me"; answers their accusations, "You say that I am" and "You have said so", "Is that your own idea or did others talk to you about me", "I have spoken openly to the world; why question me? Ask those who heard me. Surely they know what I said", "If I said something wrong, testify to what is wrong. But if I spoke truth, why did you strike me?", "My kingdom is not of this world", "You say that I am king. In fact, the reason I was born and came into the world is to testify to the truth. Everyone on the side of truth listens to me", and "Father forgive them for they know not what they do."

Jesus has spoken and demonstrated the truths he came to confirm, there is nothing left to say except to demonstrate that the authorities of earthly kingdoms are not above the one authority which governs life and death, that man's laws do not rule God's love, which transcends all.

Our Prayer: *Lord, help to see and believe what most cannot, to hear and follow the path others do not that forgoes life to surpass death, to seek and share the seeds you have sown, so that we may live in, of and through your love.*

29. *See & believe* (for if you do not there is only desolation and despair in the darkness)	30. *Hear & Follow* (the path of 'abundant love given' lights the way, if offered to others)	31. *Seek & Share* (feed faith in forgiveness through the truth of expressed mercy, charity and love)	32. Praise & Pray (cease our constant striving in the silence that is sacred, embracing and being embraced by your love)

Lessons 33

Resurrection and Salvation

Appendix A. Small Group Process: *Paired-Learning*

Optimizing Small Group Process in Studying the Gospels: *Paired-Learning*

Over the past twelve years we have refined a more efficient and effective small group process for studying Scripture. Well we would like to say that pairing group members is a new concept, it is not. However, shifting who is paired with whom over time and how we have refined the pairing-into partnering process is most innovative and quite different than the old, dated business training models that are more typically used.

The main action in the Old Testament is described is well-known and lesser-known pairings. Jesus declares his pairing with his Father, God. And Jesus selects and sends out disciples in pairs. On the next few pages you have these pairings named and pivotal Scripture offered. Thus, we feel we have a solid foundation for proposing to you that there is a better process than you may have been using, to study the content we have structured for you. We are quite pleased to offer you both a new structure for the content and a new process for engaging that content with one another.

So, peruse the listing of pairs, Scripture about Jesus pairing with his Father, and Jesus pairing and sending out disciples, in the next few pages. Then review our outline of how to pair members and operate each small group gathering in a manner that optimizes pairing and maximizes learning! Enjoy!!

Two Sons

Cain and Seth
Judah and Joseph
Rueben and Judah

Cain and Abel
Ham and Shem
Jacob and Esau
Simeon and Levi
Moses and Aaron

Terah's sons, Abraham and Nahor   Eber's sons, Peleg and Joktan
Joseph's son, Manessah and Ephraim   Judah's sons, Perez and Zerah
Moses's sons, Eleazar and Gershom   Naomi's 2 sons who died in Moab
Eli's sons, Hophni and Phinehas   Moab and Ammon
Ishmael and Isaac (2 of Abraham's 9)

5 pairs of brothers, Genesis, younger son was chosen rather than the firstborn

Seth [Cain]
Abram (Abraham)[Haran]
Issac [Ishmael]
Jacob [Esau]
Joseph [Reuben]
Ephraim [Mannaseh]

Other Male Pairs
Joshua & Caleb
Paul & Silas
Paul & Barnabas
David & Jonathan
Eli & Samuel
David & Goliath
Isaac & Ishmael

Father-Son Pairs
Adam and Abel/Cain
Abraham and Isaac
Jacob and Joseph
Noah & Ham
Moses and Eleazor/Gershom
David and Solomon
Joseph and Jesus

Paired Twelve Disciples
Peter & Andrew
James & John
Phillip & Bartholomew
Matthew & Thomas
James & Thaddeus
Simon & Judas

Couples

Adam & Eve
Samson & Delilah
Abraham & Sarah
Aquila & Priscilla
Jacob and Leah
Isaac and Rebekah
Er and Tamar
David & Bathseba
Ruth & Boaz
Aaron and Elisaheba
Amran and Jochebed
Ananias & Sapphira
Abraham and Keturah
Moses and Zipporah
Zachariah & Elizabeth
Joseph & Mary
Nahor and Milcah
Joseph and Asenath
Esau and Basemath
Lamech and Zillah

Female Pairs

Merab & Michal
Moses' mother & sister
Mary & Martha
Naaman's wife & her attendant
Ruth & Naomi
Ruth & Orpah
Joash's unnamed nurse & Pharoah's daughter
Sarah & Hagar
Jehosheba & Athaliah
Deborah & Jael
Rachel & Leah
Hannah & Peninnah
Miriam & unnamed Cushite woman
Wife of Jephthah's father & prostitute
Lamech's wives
Esther & Vashti (Hegai)
Two prostitutes appearing before King Solomon
Woman whose son was consumed & one wasn't (2 Kings 6:26-30)

The Father and the Son: *Jesus is Paired with God*

The first and primary pairing in the New Testament is of the Son of Man with God the Father:

John 1:18
No one has ever seen God, but the one and only Son, who is himself God and is in closest relationship with the Father, has made him known.

John 5:18
For this reason they tried all the more to kill him; not only was he breaking the Sabbath, but he was even calling God his own Father, making himself equal with God.

John 8:16
But if I do judge, my decisions are true, because I am not alone. I stand with the Father, who sent me.

John 14:16
And I will ask the Father, and he will give you another advocate to help you and be with you forever—

John 14:23
Jesus replied, "Anyone who loves me will obey my teaching. My Father will love them, and we will come to them and make our home with them.

John 17:5
And now, Father, glorify me in your presence with the glory I had with you before the world began.

John 17:24
Father, I want those you have given me to be with me where I am, and to see my glory, the glory you have given me because you loved me before the creation of the world.

John 20:21
Again Jesus said, "Peace be with you! As the Father has sent me, I am sending you."

Jesus Pairs His Disciples

Mark 6:7-13

Then Jesus went around teaching from village to village. Calling the Twelve to him, he began to send them out ***two by two*** and gave them authority over impure spirits. These were his instructions: "Take nothing for the journey except a staff—no bread, no bag, no money in your belts. Wear sandals but not an extra shirt. Whenever you enter a house, stay there until you leave that town. And if any place will not welcome you or listen to you, leave that place and shake the dust off your feet as a testimony against them." They went out and preached that people should repent. They drove out many demons and anointed many sick people with oil and healed them.

Matthew 4: 18-22

As Jesus was walking beside the Sea of Galilee, he saw two brothers, Simon called Peter and his brother Andrew. They were casting a net into the lake, for they were fishermen. "Come, follow me," Jesus said, "and I will send you out to fish for people." At once they left their nets and followed him. Going on from there, he saw two other brothers, James son of Zebedee and his brother John. They were in a boat with their father Zebedee, preparing their nets. Jesus called them, and immediately they left the boat and their father and followed him.

Matthew 10:1-4

Jesus called his twelve disciples to him and gave them authority to drive out impure spirits and to heal every disease and sickness. These are the names of the twelve apostles: first, Simon (who is called Peter) and his brother Andrew; James son of Zebedee, and his brother John; Philip and Bartholomew; Thomas and Matthew the tax collector; James son of Alphaeus, and Thaddaeus; Simon the Zealot and Judas Iscariot, who betrayed him.

Luke 10: 1-22

After this the Lord appointed seventy-two others and sent them ***two by two*** ahead of him to every town and place where he was about to go... "When you enter a house, first say, 'Peace to this house.' ..."When you enter a town and are welcomed, eat what is offered to you. Heal the sick who are there and tell them, 'The kingdom of God has come near to you.' ... "Whoever listens to you listens to me; ... The seventy-two returned with joy and said, "Lord, even the demons submit to us in your name." ... At that time Jesus, full of joy through the Holy Spirit, said, "I praise you, Father, Lord of heaven and earth, because you have hidden these things from the wise and learned, and revealed them to little children. Yes, Father, for this is what you were pleased to do. "All things have been committed to me by my Father. No one knows who the Son is except the Father, and no one knows who the Father is except the Son and those to whom the Son chooses to reveal him."

Appendix B. ***Four by Four Pattern Evident in the Parables of Jesus***

Four by Four Pattern Also Evident in the 'Little Stories' of Jesus

The Catholic Encyclopedia lists 33 parables. The NIV Study Bible lists 40, although five appear in different gospels in different forms. David Ahl leans to the NIV Study Bible list of 40 plus the five additional ones that Jesus told at other times in a different form, plus one in John for a total count of 46. Christina and I found that 16 key 'little stories' Jesus told are located in the first sixteen lessons of this study guide. It turns out these 16 stories conform to the four by four pattern in that they cluster naturally into 4 groups of four stories each that provide a coherent sequence and progression of meaning within and across each group. Indeed, when we studied the second set of lessons (17-32), we found 16 key parables or little stories that showed this same four by four design, a patterning that greatly furthered our understanding and insight, given they displayed a continued sequencing and progression of meaning and suggested application of principles taught by Jesus, that built and extended the first set of little stories.

It was rather remarkable, no, amazing, that our simple study suggested to us 32 lessons in two sets of sixteen, within which there were 32 little stories that seemed to arrange themselves in similar fashion of two sets of sixteen! Now, looking at these little stories arranged in clusters of four and two sets of sixteen, it seems so clear and simple ... and incredibly helpful. Yet, there seemed to be a variety of these little stories left over.

So, we gathered up the remaining little stories and arranged them in the manner we had found to be so helpful and they just seemed to fall into place. On top of that, the first cluster of 'leftover' stories seemed to introduce everything and the last cluster of leftover stories seem to conclude everything, while the middle two clusters of leftover stories outlined what was to come in the primary 32 lessons and 32 stories of the main study. It was as if someone had written a technical manual and given us an introductory outline to orient the learner to the lessons in the main study. So that is where we have placed these four groups of four stories, here at the beginning as an orientation to the whole study before you even begin it!

So, do not worry about this four by four patterning, just read the following stories with our brief reflections. See if this makes sense to you, that ideas seem to build upon one another in an accumulating sort of way. After reading these sixteen little stories in their proper order, perhaps you will be prepared for the main study in a unique fashion, that is, you will be able to catch the rhythm and cadence of the masterful method of Jesus and deepen your connection to the Holy Spirit in a special way.

As you read these stories we have placed in brackets the same or similar story as told by a different Gospel writer, and, in a couple of instances, Old Testament scripture that illuminates the little story in some way [also in brackets]. Please enjoy these little stories told by Jesus! We hope our brief reflections help you reflect in meaningful ways for your self, as well.

First Cluster of Four Introductory Stories: *Light for the World*

(1)

[Genesis 1: 1-4 In the beginning God created the heavens and the earth. Now the earth was formless and empty, darkness was over the surface of the deep, and the Spirit of God was hovering over the waters. And God said, "Let there be light," and there was light. God saw that the light was good, and he separated the light from the darkness.]

John 1:1-5 In the beginning was the Word, and the Word was with God, and the Word was God. He was with God in the beginning. Through him all things were made; without him nothing was made that has been made. In him was life, and that life was the light of all mankind. The light shines in the darkness, and the darkness has not overcome it.

(2)

Matthew 6: 22-23 "The eye is the lamp of the body. If your eyes are healthy, your whole body will be full of light. But if your eyes are unhealthy, your whole body will be full of darkness. If then the light within you is darkness, how great is that darkness!

[Luke 11: 32-36 "No one lights a lamp and puts it in a place where it will be hidden, or under a bowl. Instead they put it on its stand, so that those who come in may see the light. Your eye is the lamp of your body. When your eyes are healthy, your whole body also is full of light. But when they are unhealthy, your body also is full of darkness. See to it, then, that the light within you is not darkness. Therefore, if your whole body is full of light, and no part of it dark, it will be just as full of light as when a lamp shines its light on you."]

(3)

Matthew 5:14-16 "You are the light of the world. A town built on a hill cannot be hidden. Neither do people light a lamp and put it under a bowl. Instead they put it on its stand, and it gives light to everyone in the house. In the same way, let your light shine before others, that they may see your good deeds and glorify your Father in heaven.

[Mark 4: 21-23 He said to them, "Do you bring in a lamp to put it under a bowl or a bed? Instead, don't you put it on its stand? For whatever is hidden is meant to be disclosed, and whatever is concealed is meant to be brought out into the open. If anyone has ears to hear, let them hear."]

[Luke 8: 16-18 "No one lights a lamp and hides it in a clay jar or puts it under a bed. Instead, they put it on a stand, so that those who come in can see the light. For there is nothing hidden that will not be disclosed, and nothing concealed that will not be known or brought out into the open. Therefore consider carefully how you listen. Whoever has will be given more; whoever does not have, even what they think they have will be taken from them."]

(4)

John 12: 35-41 Then Jesus told them, "You are going to have the light just a little while longer. Walk while you have the light, before darkness overtakes you. Whoever walks in the dark does not know where they are going. Believe in the light while you have the light, so that you may become children of light." When he had finished speaking, Jesus left and hid himself from them. Even after Jesus had performed so many signs in their presence, they still would not believe in him. This was to fulfill the word of Isaiah the prophet: "Lord, who has believed our message and to whom has the arm of the Lord been revealed?" For this reason they could not believe, because, as Isaiah says elsewhere: "He has blinded their eyes and hardened their hearts, so they can neither see with their eyes, nor understand with their hearts, nor turn—and I would heal them." Isaiah said this because he saw Jesus' glory and spoke about him.

[Luke 8: 9-10 His disciples asked him what this parable meant. He said, "The knowledge of the secrets of the kingdom of God has been given to you, but to others I speak in parables, so that, "'though seeing, they may not see; though hearing, they may not understand.']

[Daniel 2:21-23 He changes times and seasons; he deposes kings and raises up others. He gives wisdom to the wise and knowledge to the discerning.
He reveals deep and hidden things; he knows what lies in darkness, and light dwells with him. I thank and praise you, God of my ancestors: You have given me wisdom and power, you have made known to me what we asked of you, you have made known to us the dream of the king."]

[Luke 10: 1, 17, 21-24 After this the Lord appointed seventy-two others and sent them two by two ahead of him to every town and place where he was about to go. The seventy-two returned with joy and said, "Lord, even the demons submit to us in your name." At that time Jesus, full of joy through the Holy Spirit, said, "I praise you, Father, Lord of heaven and earth, because you have hidden these things from the wise and learned, and revealed them to little children. Yes, Father, for this is what you were pleased to do. "All things have been committed to me by my Father. No one knows who the Son is except the Father, and no one knows who the Father is except the Son and those to whom the Son chooses to reveal him." Then he turned to his disciples and said privately, "Blessed are the eyes that see what you see. For I tell you that many prophets and kings wanted to see what you see but did not see it, and to hear what you hear but did not hear it."]

Our Reflections

These first four little stories begin the sequence and progression at the beginning – stating that there is light, the light may be taken in and given out through the heart, and that there is light for future generations of hearts in these little stories, as follows ...

Genesis and John let it be known that in the beginning was the Word and the Word was with God, that the Word was light and light was to become love incarnate, shared with all. What is not light is darkness.

+ Light or darkness may be taken in with the eyes of the heart.

+ If a heart has eyes and ears to let in the light and dispel the darkness, the light is not to be hidden or concealed; it is good and right for that light to be shone for others to see and hear in their hearts, as well.

+ Believe in the light, become children of light, for there are those whose hearts have been hardened who cannot see or hear the light in these little stories.

Your Reflections and Notes

Second Cluster of Four Introductory Stories: *In the Care of the Father*

Matthew 6:25-34 "Therefore I tell you, do not worry about your life, what you will eat or drink; or about your body, what you will wear. Is not life more than food, and the body more than clothes? Look at the birds of the air; they do not sow or reap or store away in barns, and yet your heavenly Father feeds them. Are you not much more valuable than they? Can any one of you by worrying add a single hour to your life? "And why do you worry about clothes? See how the flowers of the field grow. They do not labor or spin. Yet I tell you that not even Solomon in all his splendor was dressed like one of these. If that is how God clothes the grass of the field, which is here today and tomorrow is thrown into the fire, will he not much more clothe you—you of little faith? So do not worry, saying, 'What shall we eat?' or 'What shall we drink?' or 'What shall we wear?' For the pagans run after all these things, and your heavenly Father knows that you need them. *But seek first his kingdom and his righteousness, and all these things will be given to you as well. Therefore do not worry about tomorrow, for tomorrow will worry about itself. Each day has enough trouble of its own.*

Luke 12: 22-34 Then Jesus said to his disciples: "Therefore I tell you, do not worry about your life, what you will eat; or about your body, what you will wear. For life is more than food, and the body more than clothes. Consider the ravens: They do not sow or reap, they have no storeroom or barn; yet God feeds them. And how much more valuable you are than birds! Who of you by worrying can add a single hour to your life? Since you cannot do this very little thing, why do you worry about the rest? "Consider how the wild flowers grow. They do not labor or spin. Yet I tell you, not even Solomon in all his splendor was dressed like one of these. If that is how God clothes the grass of the field, which is here today, and tomorrow is thrown into the fire, how much more will he clothe you—you of little faith! And do not set your heart on what you will eat or drink; do not worry about it. For the pagan world runs after all such things, and your Father knows that you need them. But seek his kingdom, and these things will be given to you as well. *"Do not be afraid, little flock, for your Father has been pleased to give you the kingdom. Sell your possessions and give to the poor. Provide purses for yourselves that will not wear out, a treasure in heaven that will never fail, where no thief comes near and no moth destroys. For where your treasure is, there your heart will be also.*

Matthew 10: 5-8, 16 These twelve Jesus sent out with the following instructions: "Do not go among the Gentiles or enter any town of the Samaritans. Go rather to the lost sheep of Israel. As you go, proclaim this message: 'The kingdom of heaven has come near.' Heal the sick, raise the dead, cleanse those who have leprosy, drive out demons. Freely you have received; freely give. *"I am sending you out like sheep among wolves. Therefore be as shrewd as snakes and as innocent as doves.*

Matthew 8: 18-20 When Jesus saw the crowd around him, he gave orders to cross to the other side of the lake. Then a teacher of the law came to him and said, "Teacher, I will follow you wherever you go." Jesus replied, *"Foxes have dens and birds have nests, but the Son of Man has no place to lay his head."*

Our Reflections

This second cluster of four little stories begins by pointing out that we are in our Father's care and do not have to be afraid or to worry about food, water, clothes and shelter. In the first story he lets us know that He has given the light - the earthly body and bread, the water and blood that is wine, the very breath and word that leads to the kingdom of heaven – to us in the gift of his son. The second story points out this gift allows us to sell and give away all worldly material possessions and concerns and seek this kingdom of heaven. And in the third story, in innocence, with this gift of light and love, he sends us out as disciples, recognizing the difference between people with hardened, closed hearts and those whose hearts are softly open to share this treasure from and of heaven. Finally in the last story we find that in the end we may rest and be comforted because Jesus took upon himself all the darkness and death the world had to offer, without rest or reprieve, until he was laid to rest only to rise again.

Your Reflections and Notes

Third Cluster: *Come as Little Children to Me and to the Kingdom of Heaven*

Matthew 7: 7-12 "Ask and it will be given to you; seek and you will find; knock and the door will be opened to you. For everyone who asks receives; the one who seeks finds; and to the one who knocks, the door will be opened. "Which of you, if your son asks for bread, will give him a stone? Or if he asks for a fish, will give him a snake? If you, then, though you are evil, know how to give good gifts to your children, how much more will your Father in heaven give good gifts to those who ask him! So in everything, do to others what you would have them do to you, for this sums up the Law and the Prophets.

[Luke 11: 9-13 "So I say to you: Ask and it will be given to you; seek and you will find; knock and the door will be opened to you. For everyone who asks receives; the one who seeks finds; and to the one who knocks, the door will be opened. "Which of you fathers, if your son asks for a fish, will give him a snake instead? Or if he asks for an egg, will give him a scorpion? If you then, though you are evil, know how to give good gifts to your children, how much more will your Father in heaven give the Holy Spirit to those who ask him!"]

Matthew 18:1-5 At that time the disciples came to Jesus and asked, "Who, then, is the greatest in the kingdom of heaven?" He called a little child to him, and placed the child among them. And he said: "Truly I tell you, unless you change and become like little children, you will never enter the kingdom of heaven. Therefore, whoever takes the lowly position of this child is the greatest in the kingdom of heaven. And whoever welcomes one such child in my name welcomes me.

[Mark 9: 33-36 They came to Capernaum. When he was in the house, he asked them, "What were you arguing about on the road?" But they kept quiet because on the way they had argued about who was the greatest. Sitting down, Jesus called the Twelve and said, "Anyone who wants to be first must be the very last, and the servant of all." He took a little child whom he placed among them. Taking the child in his arms, he said to them, "Whoever welcomes one of these little children in my name welcomes me; and whoever welcomes me does not welcome me but the one who sent me."]

Matthew 18: 6-9 "If anyone causes one of these little ones—those who believe in me—to stumble, it would be better for them to have a large millstone hung around their neck and to be drowned in the depths of the sea. Woe to the world because of the things that cause people to stumble! Such things must come, but woe to the person through whom they come! If your hand or your foot causes you to stumble, cut it off and throw it away. It is better for you to enter life maimed or crippled than to have two hands or two feet and be thrown into eternal fire. And if your eye causes you to stumble, gouge it out and throw it away. It is better for you to enter life with one eye than to have two eyes and be thrown into the fire of hell.

Matthew 19: 13-14 Then people brought little children to Jesus for him to place his hands on them and pray for them. But the disciples rebuked them. Jesus said, "Let the little children come to me, and do not hinder them, for the kingdom of heaven belongs to such as these." When he had placed his hands on them, he went on from there.

[*Mark 10: 13-16* People were bringing little children to Jesus for him to place his hands on them, but the disciples rebuked them. When Jesus saw this, he was indignant. He said to them, "Let the little children come to me, and do not hinder them, for the kingdom of God belongs to such as these. Truly I tell you, anyone who will not receive the kingdom of God like a little child will never enter it." And he took the children in his arms, placed his hands on them and blessed them.[

[*Luke 18: 15-17* People were also bringing babies to Jesus for him to place his hands on them. When the disciples saw this, they rebuked them. But Jesus called the children to him and said, "Let the little children come to me, and do not hinder them, for the kingdom of God belongs to such as these. Truly I tell you, anyone who will not receive the kingdom of God like a little child will never enter it."]

Our Reflections

The Father gives his Son and his Son gives to us, his little children, what God has given his Son. For if we who are evil give good things to our children what might the Father and the Son, who are good and full of light, be capable of giving to their children (us)?

So we must become like little children. We must welcome the Son as the Son has welcomed all that the Father has given him. The Son has given these gifts to us, his children, that we might come into a state of being that readies us to enter the Kingdom of Heaven

Any who hinder the children of light, the children of the father and the Son, will be destroyed.

Indeed, the kingdom of heaven belongs to the children.

Your Reflections and Notes

The Fourth and Final Cluster of Four Stories: *Enter the Kingdom of Heaven*

Matthew 24: 32-35 <u>The Lesson of the Fig Tree</u>
"From the fig tree learn its lesson: as soon as its branch becomes tender and puts out its leaves, you know that summer is near. So also, when you see all these things, you know that he is near, at the very gates. Truly, I say to you, this generation will not pass away until all these things take place. Heaven and earth will pass away, but my words will not pass away.

Matthew 25: 1-13 <u>The Parable of the Ten Virgins</u>
"At that time the kingdom of heaven will be like ten virgins who took their lamps and went out to meet the bridegroom. Five of them were foolish and five were wise. The foolish ones took their lamps but did not take any oil with them. The wise ones, however, took oil in jars along with their lamps. The bridegroom was a long time in coming, and they all became drowsy and fell asleep. "At midnight the cry rang out: 'Here's the bridegroom! Come out to meet him!' "Then all the virgins woke up and trimmed their lamps. The foolish ones said to the wise, 'Give us some of your oil; our lamps are going out.' "'No,' they replied, 'there may not be enough for both us and you. Instead, go to those who sell oil and buy some for yourselves.' "But while they were on their way to buy the oil, the bridegroom arrived. The virgins who were ready went in with him to the wedding banquet. And the door was shut.
"Later the others also came. 'Lord, Lord,' they said, 'open the door for us!'
"But he replied, 'Truly I tell you, I don't know you.'
"Therefore keep watch, because you do not know the day or the hour.

Matthew 25: 14-23 <u>The Parable of the Bags of Gold</u>
"Again, it will be like a man going on a journey, who called his servants and entrusted his wealth to them. To one he gave five bags of gold, to another two bags, and to another one bag, each according to his ability. Then he went on his journey. The man who had received five bags of gold went at once and put his money to work and gained five bags more. So also, the one with two bags of gold gained two more. But the man who had received one bag went off, dug a hole in the ground and hid his master's money. "After a long time the master of those servants returned and settled accounts with them. The man who had received five bags of gold brought the other five. 'Master,' he said, 'you entrusted me with five bags of gold. See, I have gained five more.'
"His master replied, 'Well done, good and faithful servant! You have been faithful with a few things; I will put you in charge of many things. Come and share your master's happiness!'
"The man with two bags of gold also came. 'Master,' he said, 'you entrusted me with two bags of gold; see, I have gained two more.'
"His master replied, 'Well done, good and faithful servant! You have been faithful with a few things; I will put you in charge of many things. Come and share your master's happiness!'
"Then the man who had received one bag of gold came. 'Master,' he said, 'I knew

that you are a hard man, harvesting where you have not sown and gathering where you have not scattered seed. **25** So I was afraid and went out and hid your gold in the ground. See, here is what belongs to you.'

"His master replied, 'You wicked, lazy servant! So you knew that I harvest where I have not sown and gather where I have not scattered seed? Well then, you should have put my money on deposit with the bankers, so that when I returned I would have received it back with interest. "'So take the bag of gold from him and give it to the one who has ten bags. For whoever has will be given more, and they will have an abundance. Whoever does not have, even what they have will be taken from them. And throw that worthless servant outside, into the darkness, where there will be weeping and gnashing of teeth.'

Matthew 25: 31-46 <u>The Sheep and the Goats</u>
"When the Son of Man comes in his glory, and all the angels with him, he will sit on his glorious throne. All the nations will be gathered before him, and he will separate the people one from another as a shepherd separates the sheep from the goats. He will put the sheep on his right and the goats on his left. "Then the King will say to those on his right, 'Come, you who are blessed by my Father; take your inheritance, the kingdom prepared for you since the creation of the world. For I was hungry and you gave me something to eat, I was thirsty and you gave me something to drink, I was a stranger and you invited me in, I needed clothes and you clothed me, I was sick and you looked after me, I was in prison and you came to visit me.'

"Then the righteous will answer him, 'Lord, when did we see you hungry and feed you, or thirsty and give you something to drink? When did we see you a stranger and invite you in, or needing clothes and clothe you? When did we see you sick or in prison and go to visit you?'

"The King will reply, 'Truly I tell you, whatever you did for one of the least of these brothers and sisters of mine, you did for me.'

"Then he will say to those on his left, 'Depart from me, you who are cursed, into the eternal fire prepared for the devil and his angels. For I was hungry and you gave me nothing to eat, I was thirsty and you gave me nothing to drink, I was a stranger and you did not invite me in, I needed clothes and you did not clothe me, I was sick and in prison and you did not look after me.'

"They also will answer, 'Lord, when did we see you hungry or thirsty or a stranger or needing clothes or sick or in prison, and did not help you?'

"He will reply, 'Truly I tell you, whatever you did not do for one of the least of these, you did not do for me.'

"Then they will go away to eternal punishment, but the righteous to eternal life."

Our Reflections

In the first little story, the tender shoots of everlasting life foretell the coming of the Lord in the Kingdom of Heaven.

In the second little story we are cautioned further - that the Lord is coming and there are some who are not prepared and who are asleep; the door will be closed to the feast and they will be left outside.

In the third little story we are given the details of what we must do and what will happen if we do not - Such gifts and blessings, sufferings and severities, given in different measure to different men and women, are meant to become the treasures of the heart for others, shared generously in order to increase the harvest of the Lord. Those gifts of light and love that are withheld are squandered in the eyes of the heart of the Lord, and those who squander such treasure as they have been given will be thrown out into the darkness where the light of love does not shine.

And the final and fourth little story completes the sequence by telling us that as the Lord has given all people the bread of his body, the water and wine of his heart, the breath and Word of his Holy Spirit, as well as his perfect innocence and love in the giving of his earthly life in order to defeat and destroy death, so too does the Lord charge each and all of us to salve the hunger, quench the thirst, comfort those in disease and despair with these same gifts he has given to us. At the end of times and the beginning of eternity, when we are all gathered together for the last time, we will be separated to the right and to the left. For those who have not fed, watered and comforted others, they will be without life, and for those who have done so there is eternal life.

So it is that these sixteen stories simply and clearly, in an amazing four by four design, outline the lessons and stories to follow: That light comes into the world, that this light takes care of all, that if we come as children into the light the light will be in us and we will be in the light, and, finally, that receiving, offering, sharing and embracing the light is the portal into the kingdom of heaven.

Your Reflections and Notes

Appendix C. God's Cluster (Lessons 1-4): *Fire, Earth, Water, Air, Fire*

Angels

God's Cluster (Lessons 1-4):

Fire, Earth, Water, Air, Fire

Explore the nature of the gift(s) made manifest within and across the pattern of these four motifs: *What is the Gift that God gave to the world and how did He do so?*

(Fire ... angelic beings)

Angels came to Zachariah and Elizabeth, Mary and Joseph; angels came to the shepherds near Bethlehem at the birth of Jesus; angels came to Joseph sending him to and from Egypt; angels tended to Jesus after his testing in the wilderness by Satan.

(Earth ... stone, bread)

Joseph and Mary came to Bethlehem, then to Egypt, then to Nazareth with Jesus, and then Jesus went into the wilderness alone.

And in the wilderness, Satan tested Jesus with creating bread from stone, casting himself down upon the stones to be raised up by angels, with all the kingdoms of earth as king, and then left him in the wilderness alone.

(Water ... wine, blood)

Both Elizabeth's and Mary's water broke open releasing, carrying John and Jesus into the world, Jesus shed his blood and was washed during his naming and circumcision ceremony, Jesus was baptized with water by John, and Jesus changed water into wine at the wedding in Canaan.

(Air ... breath, wings, words)

Each time during Passover, Jesus was carried to the Temple in Jerusalem as a baby to be named and circumcised, as a twelve year old stayed to ask questions and teach, as a man to clear out the moneychangers, and, finally to say little as a sacrifice and gift.

Doves were present at his birth, at his circumcision, at his baptism and at the clearing of the Temple.

(Fire ... spirit)

The Holy Spirit was placed into John through Elizabeth and Zachariah; the Holy Spirit came upon Mary and was with Jesus; the Holy Spirit came to Simeon and Anna; the Holy Spirit came down upon Jesus at his baptism.

Angels

(1) Luke 1: 11-20 Then an angel of the Lord appeared to him, standing at the right side of the altar of incense. When Zechariah saw him, he was startled and was gripped with fear. But the angel said to him: "Do not be afraid, Zechariah; your prayer has been heard. Your wife Elizabeth will bear you a son, and you are to call him John. He will be a joy and delight to you, and many will rejoice because of his birth, for he will be great in the sight of the Lord. He is never to take wine or other fermented drink, and he will be filled with the Holy Spirit even before he is born. He will bring back many of the people of Israel to the Lord their God. And he will go on before the Lord, in the spirit and power of Elijah, to turn the hearts of the parents to their children and the disobedient to the wisdom of the righteous—to make ready a people prepared for the Lord."
Zechariah asked the angel, "How can I be sure of this? I am an old man and my wife is well along in years." The angel said to him, "I am Gabriel. I stand in the presence of God, and I have been sent to speak to you and to tell you this good news. And now you will be silent and not able to speak until the day this happens, because you did not believe my words, which will come true at their appointed time."

(1) Luke 1: 26-38 In the sixth month of Elizabeth's pregnancy, God sent the angel Gabriel to Nazareth, a town in Galilee, to a virgin pledged to be married to a man named Joseph, a descendant of David. The virgin's name was Mary. The angel went to her and said, "Greetings, you who are highly favored! The Lord is with you." Mary was greatly troubled at his words and wondered what kind of greeting this might be. But the angel said to her, "Do not be afraid, Mary; you have found favor with God. You will conceive and give birth to a son, and you are to call him Jesus. He will be great and will be called the Son of the Most High. The Lord God will give him the throne of his father David, and he will reign over Jacob's descendants forever; his kingdom will never end."
"How will this be," Mary asked the angel, "since I am a virgin?" The angel answered, "The Holy Spirit will come on you, and the power of the Most High will overshadow you. So the holy one to be born will be called the Son of God. Even Elizabeth your relative is going to have a child in her old age, and she who was said to be unable to conceive is in her sixth month. For no word from God will ever fail."
"I am the Lord's servant," Mary answered. "May your word to me be fulfilled." Then the angel left her.

(2) Matthew 1: 20-21 But after he had considered this, an angel of the Lord appeared to him in a dream and said, "Joseph son of David, do not be afraid to take Mary home as your wife, because what is conceived in her is from the Holy Spirit. She will give birth to a son, and you are to give him the name Jesus, because he will save his people from their sins."

(3) Luke 2: 8-15 And there were shepherds living out in the fields nearby, keeping watch over their flocks at night. An angel of the Lord appeared to them, and the glory of the Lord shone around them, and they were terrified. But the angel said to them, "Do not be afraid. I bring you good news that will cause great joy for all the people. Today in the town of David a Savior has been born to you; he is the Messiah, the Lord. This will be a sign to you: You will find a baby wrapped in cloths and lying in a manger." Suddenly a great company of the heavenly host appeared with the angel, praising God and saying,

"Glory to God in the highest heaven,
  and on earth peace to those on whom his favor rests."

When the angels had left them and gone into heaven, the shepherds said to one another, "Let's go to Bethlehem and see this thing that has happened, which the Lord has told us about."

(2) Matthew 2: 12-13; 19-22 And having been warned in a dream not to go back to Herod, they returned to their country by another route.
When they had gone, an angel of the Lord appeared to Joseph in a dream. "Get up," he said, "take the child and his mother and escape to Egypt. Stay there until I tell you, for Herod is going to search for the child to kill him."
So he got up, took the child and his mother during the night and left for Egypt, where he stayed until the death of Herod.
After Herod died, an angel of the Lord appeared in a dream to Joseph in Egypt and said, "Get up, take the child and his mother and go to the land of Israel, for those who were trying to take the child's life are dead."
So he got up, took the child and his mother and went to the land of Israel. But when he heard that Archelaus was reigning in Judea in place of his father Herod, he was afraid to go there. Having been warned in a dream, he withdrew to the district of Galilee, and he went and lived in a town called Nazareth.

(4) Matthew 4: 11 Then the devil left him, and angels came and attended him.

Question: What do you make of the general pattern that an angel from God greets the person visited, comforts and calms their fear, gives good news, directs them to a specific action, and then either corrects their response or encourages them in their faith that God's Word is true, as predictions are made as to what will happen as a consequence of these gifts? What are the messages of the angels sent by God?

Places of Earth

(1) Luke 1:39; At that time Mary got ready and hurried to a town in the hill country of Judea, where she entered Zechariah's home and greeted Elizabeth. Mary stayed with Elizabeth for about three months and then returned home.

(2) Luke 2:1-4 In those days Caesar Augustus issued a decree that a census should be taken of the entire Roman world. (This was the first census that took place while Quirinius was governor of Syria.) And everyone went to their own town to register. So Joseph also went up from the town of Nazareth in Galilee to Judea, to Bethlehem the town of David, because he belonged to the house and line of David.

(3) Matthew 2:14-15; 21-23 So he got up, took the child and his mother during the night and left for Egypt, where he stayed until the death of Herod. So he got up, took the child and his mother and went to the land of Israel. But when he heard that Archelaus was reigning in Judea in place of his father Herod, he was afraid to go there. Having been warned in a dream, he withdrew to the district of Galilee, and he went and lived in a town called Nazareth.

(4) Matthew 4:1 Then Jesus was led by the Spirit into the wilderness to be tempted by the devil.

Question: What patterns to you see in where God placed Jesus and his family? What were God's intentions in such placement?

Flow of Water, Blood and Wine

(1) Luke 1:57-59 When it was time for Elizabeth to have her baby, she gave birth to a son. Her neighbors and relatives heard that the Lord had shown her great mercy, and they shared her joy. On the eighth day they came to circumcise the child, and they were going to name him after his father Zechariah, but his mother spoke up and said, "No! He is to be called John."

(1) Luke 2:5-7 He went there to register with Mary, who was pledged to be married to him and was expecting a child. While they were there, the time came for the baby to be born, and she gave birth to her firstborn, a son. She wrapped him in cloths and placed him in a manger, because there was no guest room available for them.

(2) Luke 2: 21-22, 27 On the eighth day, when it was time to circumcise the child, he was named Jesus, the name the angel had given him before he was conceived. When the time came for the purification rites required by the Law of Moses, Joseph and Mary took him to Jerusalem to present him to the Lord (as it is written in the Law of the Lord, "Every firstborn male is to be consecrated to the Lord"), ... When the parents brought in the child Jesus to do for him what the custom of the Law required, ...

(3) Matthew 3: 11-17 Then Jesus came from Galilee to the Jordan to be baptized by John. As soon as Jesus was baptized, he went up out of the water.

(4) John 2: 1-10 On the third day a wedding took place at Cana in Galilee. Jesus' mother was there, and Jesus and his disciples had also been invited to the wedding. When the wine was gone, Jesus' mother said to him, "They have no more wine." "Woman, why do you involve me?" Jesus replied. "My hour has not yet come." His mother said to the servants, "Do whatever he tells you." Nearby stood six stone water jars, the kind used by the Jews for ceremonial washing, each holding from twenty to thirty gallons. Jesus said to the servants, "Fill the jars with water"; so they filled them to the brim. Then he told them, "Now draw some out and take it to the master of the banquet." They did so, and the master of the banquet tasted the water that had been turned into wine. He did not realize where it had come from, though the servants who had drawn the water knew. Then he called the bridegroom aside and said, "Everyone brings out the choice wine first and then the cheaper wine after the guests have had too much to drink; but you have saved the best till now."

Question: What do you make of the pattern of water breaking open and a woman bleeding to begin new life so the passage through birth may occur, the blood of circumcision washed off in the temple, baptizing by being submerged and coming up and out of water, and changing water into wine? What is God's meaning and preparation through this medium?

107

The Breath of God: *The wind (ruach/spirit) and the Word*

(1) Luke 1:57-59 When it was time for Elizabeth to have her baby, she gave birth to a son. Her neighbors and relatives heard that the Lord had shown her great mercy, and they shared her joy. On the eighth day they came to circumcise the child, and they were going to name him after his father Zechariah, but his mother spoke up and said, "No! He is to be called John."

Luke 2:5-7 He went there to register with Mary, who was pledged to be married to him and was expecting a child. While they were there, the time came for the baby to be born, and she gave birth to her firstborn, a son. She wrapped him in cloths and placed him in a manger, because there was no guest room available for them.

Luke 2: 21-40 When the time came for the purification rites required by the Law of Moses, Joseph and Mary took him to Jerusalem to present him to the Lord (as it is written in the Law of the Lord, "Every firstborn male is to be consecrated to the Lord"), and to offer a sacrifice in keeping with what is said in the Law of the Lord: "a pair of doves or two young pigeons."
Now there was a man in Jerusalem called Simeon, who was righteous and devout. He was waiting for the consolation of Israel, and the Holy Spirit was on him. It had been revealed to him by the Holy Spirit that he would not die before he had seen the Lord's Messiah. Moved by the Spirit, he went into the temple courts. When the parents brought in the child Jesus to do for him what the custom of the Law required, Simeon took him in his arms and praised God, saying:

"Sovereign Lord, as you have promised,
  you may now dismiss your servant in peace.
For my eyes have seen your salvation,
  which you have prepared in the sight of all nations:
a light for revelation to the Gentiles,
  and the glory of your people Israel."

The child's father and mother marveled at what was said about him. Then Simeon blessed them and said to Mary, his mother: "This child is destined to cause the falling and rising of many in Israel, and to be a sign that will be spoken against, so that the thoughts of many hearts will be revealed. And a sword will pierce your own soul too."
There was also a prophet, Anna, the daughter of Penuel, of the tribe of Asher. She was very old; she had lived with her husband seven years after her marriage, and then was a widow until she was eighty-four.[e] She never left the temple but worshiped night and day, fasting and praying. Coming up to them at that very moment, she gave thanks to God and spoke about the child to all who were looking forward to the redemption of Jerusalem.
When Joseph and Mary had done everything required by the Law of the Lord, they returned to Galilee to their own town of Nazareth. And the child grew and became strong; he was filled with wisdom, and the grace of God was on him.

(2) Luke 2: 41-51 Every year Jesus' parents went to Jerusalem for the Festival of the Passover. When he was twelve years old, they went up to the festival, according to the custom. After the festival was over, while his parents were returning home, the boy Jesus stayed behind in Jerusalem, but they were unaware of it. Thinking he was in their company, they traveled on for a day. Then they began looking for him among their relatives and friends. When they did not find him, they went back to Jerusalem to look for him. After three days they found him in the temple courts, sitting among the teachers, listening to them and asking them questions. Everyone who heard him was amazed at his understanding and his answers. When his parents saw him, they were astonished. His mother said to him, "Son, why have you treated us like this? Your father and I have been anxiously searching for you."
"Why were you searching for me?" he asked. "Didn't you know I had to be in my Father's house?" But they did not understand what he was saying to them.
Then he went down to Nazareth with them and was obedient to them. But his mother treasured all these things in her heart.

(3) Matthew 3: 13-17 Then Jesus came from Galilee to the Jordan to be baptized by John. But John tried to deter him, saying, "I need to be baptized by you, and do you come to me?"
Jesus replied, "Let it be so now; it is proper for us to do this to fulfill all righteousness." Then John consented. As soon as Jesus was baptized, he went up out of the water. At that moment heaven was opened, and he saw the Spirit of God descending like a dove and alighting on him. And a voice from heaven said, "This is my Son, whom I love; with him I am well pleased."

  John 1: 29-34 28 This all happened at Bethany on the other side of the Jordan, where John was baptizing. The next day John saw Jesus coming toward him and said, "Look, the Lamb of God, who takes away the sin of the world! This is the one I meant when I said, 'A man who comes after me has surpassed me because he was before me.' I myself did not know him, but the reason I came baptizing with water was that he might be revealed to Israel." Then John gave this testimony: "I saw the Spirit come down from heaven as a dove and remain on him. And I myself did not know him, but the one who sent me to baptize with water told me, 'The man on whom you see the Spirit come down and remain is the one who will baptize with the Holy Spirit.' I have seen and I testify that this is God's Chosen One."

(4) John 2: 13-25 When it was almost time for the Jewish Passover, Jesus went up to Jerusalem. In the temple courts he found people selling cattle, sheep and doves, and others sitting at tables exchanging money. So he made a whip out of cords, and drove all from the temple courts, both sheep and cattle; he scattered the coins of the money changers and overturned their tables. To those who sold doves he said, "Get these out of here! Stop turning my Father's house into a market!" His disciples remembered that it is written: "Zeal for your house will consume me." The Jews then responded to him, "What sign can you show us to prove your authority to do all this?" Jesus answered them, "Destroy this temple, and I will raise it again in three days." They replied, "It has taken forty-six years to build this temple, and you are going to raise it in three days?" But the temple he had spoken of was his body. After he was raised from the dead, his disciples recalled what he had said. Then they believed the scripture and the words that Jesus had spoken. Now while he was in Jerusalem at the Passover Festival, many people saw the signs he was performing and believed in his name. But Jesus would not entrust himself to them, for he knew all people. He did not need any testimony about mankind, for he knew what was in each person.

Question: *What do you make of the pattern of the spring migration of doves at the time of John's birth near Passover and the fall migration at the time of Jesus' birth in the fall 6 months later, the doves at Mary's purification and the circumcision and naming of Jesus at Passover in the Temple in Jerusalem, the teaching of the 12-year old Jesus in the Temple in Jerusalem at Passover, the baptism of Jesus by John, and the doves at the Temple in Jerusalem during Passover when Jesus cleared it? What is God's meaning and intent with the words spoken at these times and events, primarily during Passover at the Temple?*

Fire: The Incoming of the Holy Spirit

(1) Luke 1: 39-45 At that time Mary got ready and hurried to a town in the hill country of Judea, where she entered Zechariah's home and greeted Elizabeth. When Elizabeth heard Mary's greeting, the baby leaped in her womb, and Elizabeth was filled with the Holy Spirit. In a loud voice she exclaimed: "Blessed are you among women, and blessed is the child you will bear! But why am I so favored, that the mother of my Lord should come to me? As soon as the sound of your greeting reached my ears, the baby in my womb leaped for joy. Blessed is she who has believed that the Lord would fulfill his promises to her!"

(2) Luke 1: 61-80 They said to her, "There is no one among your relatives who has that name." Then they made signs to his father, to find out what he would like to name the child. He asked for a writing tablet, and to everyone's astonishment he wrote, "His name is John." Immediately his mouth was opened and his tongue set free, and he began to speak, praising God. All the neighbors were filled with awe, and throughout the hill country of Judea people were talking about all these things. Everyone who heard this wondered about it, asking, "What then is this child going to be?" For the Lord's hand was with him.

His father Zechariah was filled with the Holy Spirit and prophesied:

"Praise be to the Lord, the God of Israel,
    because he has come to his people and redeemed them.
He has raised up a horn of salvation for us
    in the house of his servant David
(as he said through his holy prophets of long ago),
    salvation from our enemies
    and from the hand of all who hate us—
to show mercy to our ancestors
    and to remember his holy covenant,
    the oath he swore to our father Abraham:
to rescue us from the hand of our enemies,
    and to enable us to serve him without fear
    in holiness and righteousness before him all our days.
And you, my child, will be called a prophet of the Most High;
    for you will go on before the Lord to prepare the way for him,
to give his people the knowledge of salvation
    through the forgiveness of their sins,
because of the tender mercy of our God,
    by which the rising sun will come to us from heaven
to shine on those living in darkness
    and in the shadow of death,
to guide our feet into the path of peace."
 And the child grew and became strong in spirit; and he lived in the wilderness until he appeared publicly to Israel.

(3) Luke 2: 21-40 When the time came for the purification rites required by the Law of Moses, Joseph and Mary took him to Jerusalem to present him to the Lord (as it is written in the Law of the Lord, "Every firstborn male is to be consecrated to the Lord"), and to offer a sacrifice in keeping with what is said in the Law of the Lord: "a pair of doves or two young pigeons."
Now there was a man in Jerusalem called Simeon, who was righteous and devout. He was waiting for the consolation of Israel, and the Holy Spirit was on him. It had been revealed to him by the Holy Spirit that he would not die before he had seen the Lord's Messiah. Moved by the Spirit, he went into the temple courts. When the parents brought in the child Jesus to do for him what the custom of the Law required, Simeon took him in his arms and praised God, saying:

"Sovereign Lord, as you have promised,
    you may now dismiss your servant in peace.
For my eyes have seen your salvation,
    which you have prepared in the sight of all nations:
a light for revelation to the Gentiles,
    and the glory of your people Israel."

The child's father and mother marveled at what was said about him. Then Simeon blessed them and said to Mary, his mother: "This child is destined to cause the falling and rising of many in Israel, and to be a sign that will be spoken against, so that the thoughts of many hearts will be revealed. And a sword will pierce your own soul too."
There was also a prophet, Anna, the daughter of Penuel, of the tribe of Asher. She was very old; she had lived with her husband seven years after her marriage, and then was a widow until she was eighty-four. She never left the temple but worshiped night and day, fasting and praying. Coming up to them at that very moment, she gave thanks to God and spoke about the child to all who were looking forward to the redemption of Jerusalem.
When Joseph and Mary had done everything required by the Law of the Lord, they returned to Galilee to their own town of Nazareth. And the child grew and became strong; he was filled with wisdom, and the grace of God was on him.

(4) Mathew 3: 11-17 "I baptize you with water for repentance. But after me comes one who is more powerful than I, whose sandals I am not worthy to carry. He will baptize you with the Holy Spirit and fire. His winnowing fork is in his hand, and he will clear his threshing floor, gathering his wheat into the barn and burning up the chaff with unquenchable fire." Then Jesus came from Galilee to the Jordan to be baptized by John. But John tried to deter him, saying, "I need to be baptized by you, and do you come to me?" Jesus replied, "Let it be so now; it is proper for us to do this to fulfill all righteousness." Then John consented.
As soon as Jesus was baptized, he went up out of the water. At that moment heaven was opened, and he saw the Spirit of God descending like a dove and alighting on him. And a voice from heaven said, "This is my Son, whom I love; with him I am well pleased."

Question: *What do you gather from the Holy Spirit entering John and Elizabeth, being in Jesus and Mary, entering Zachariah, Simeon and Anna, and descending upon Jesus at his baptism by John? What did God mean to impart in these actions?*
Explore the nature of the gift(s) made manifest within and across the pattern of these four motifs: *What is the Gift that God gave to the world?*

Explore the nature of the gift(s) made manifest within and across the pattern of these four motifs: *What is the Gift that God gave to the world?*

Appendix D. Graphics for 4 x 4 Design from Previous Publications

Graphics on the next few pages that provide the original scaffolding for perceiving the 4 x 4 design found in this study of the Gospels may be found in the following publications:

Vraniak, Damian (1990) *Parssiterns: The Parts, Processes, Principles and Patterns of Transformation*

Vraniak, D. and Mowchan, C. (2003) *Connecting with God in a Disconnected World: A Guide for Spiritual Growth and Renewal*

Vraniak, Damian (2009) *Maps & Metaphors of the Human Heart: 1,2,3-Mystery*

Vraniak, Damian (2012) *Paired-Learning for Students and Classroom Teachers*

Vraniak, Damian and Christina (2015) *Small Treasures of a Human Heart: Light Musings & Brief Illuminations of the Love Between Beauty and Truth*

Figure 1. Four layers, planes or dimensions of focus.

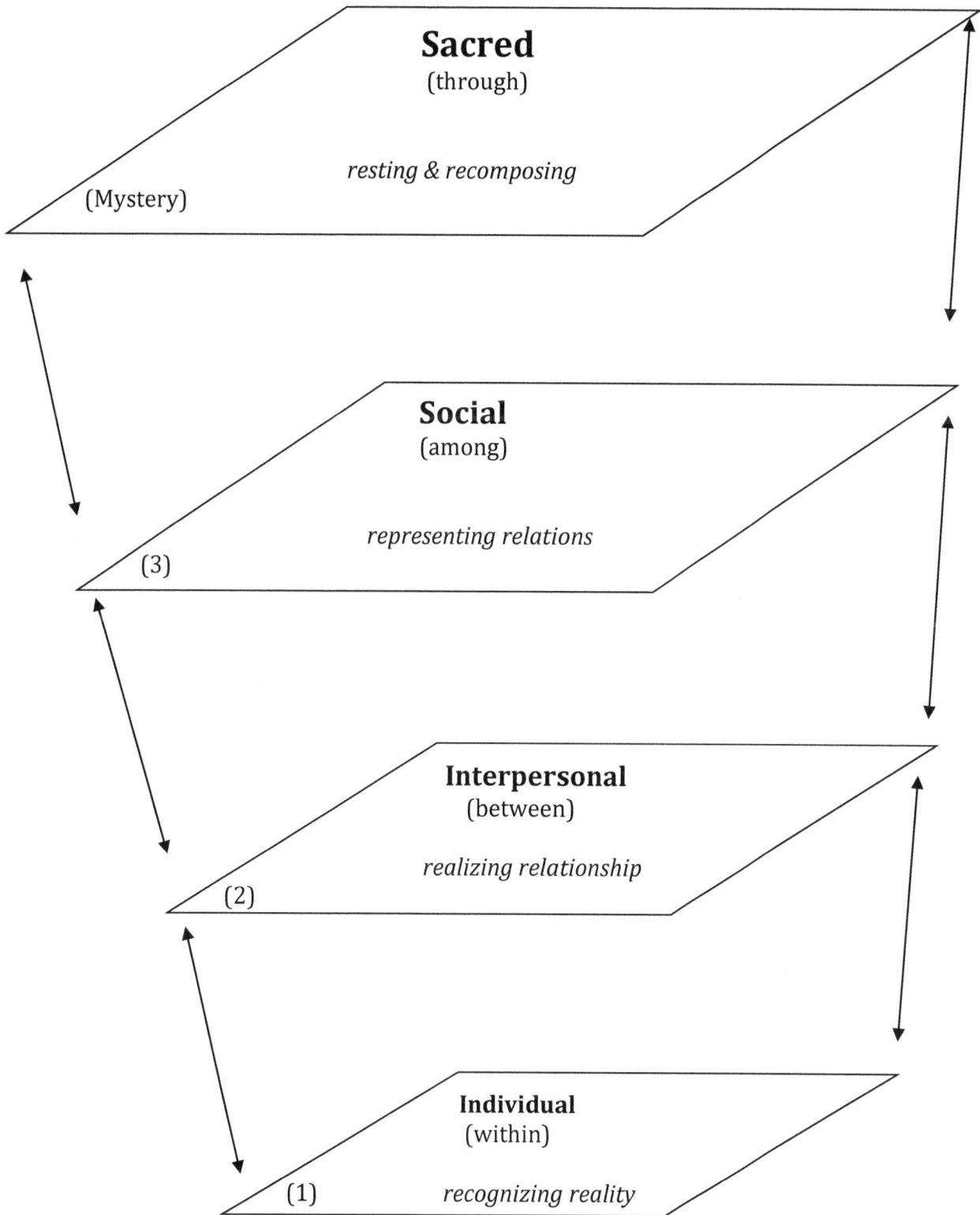

Sacred
(through)

resting & recomposing

(Mystery)

Social
(among)

representing relations

(3)

Interpersonal
(between)

realizing relationship

(2)

Individual
(within)

recognizing reality

(1)

Table 4. *Levels of Context and Primary Challenges*

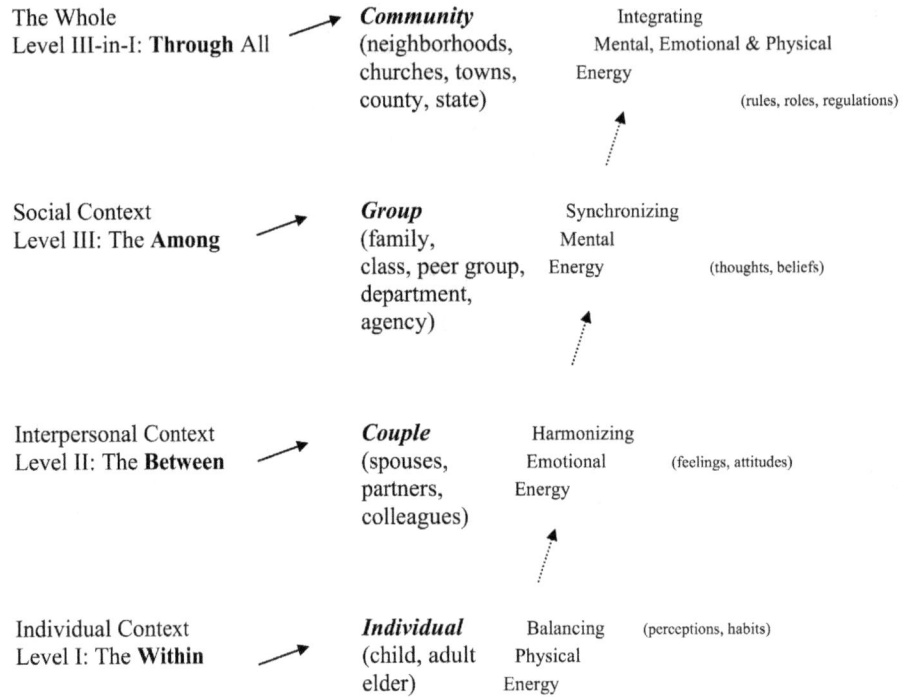

The Whole Level III-in-I: **Through** All	→ *Community* (neighborhoods, churches, towns, county, state)	Integrating Mental, Emotional & Physical Energy (rules, roles, regulations)
Social Context Level III: The **Among**	→ *Group* (family, class, peer group, department, agency)	Synchronizing Mental Energy (thoughts, beliefs)
Interpersonal Context Level II: The **Between**	→ *Couple* (spouses, partners, colleagues)	Harmonizing Emotional (feelings, attitudes) Energy
Individual Context Level I: The **Within**	→ *Individual* (child, adult elder)	Balancing (perceptions, habits) Physical Energy

---

Changing Force to Flow:	*Shaping Flow to Form:*	*Varying Form:*	*Integrating Force, Flow, Form:*
Hi to Lower Energy	Ineffective to Effective	Elaborate Variations	Transforming crisis, chaos
Hi to Lower Intensity	Inefficient to Efficient	Maximize Benefits	into calm, civility, order
Harmful to Non-harmful	*Non-Harmful to Beneficial*	*Beneficial to Many*	*Generational Legacy*

Table 1. *Maps: Four Layers and Domains of Focus*

	1	**2**	**3**	**3-in-1**
	"Within"	"Between"	"Among"	"Through"
	Individual	**Interpersonal**	**Social**	**Sacred**
Makeup	Behavioral: *Doing*	Emotional: *Feeling*	Mental: *Thinking*	Soulful: *Divining*
Mechanisms & Methods	Grow: *Increase*	Develop: *Advance*	Mature: *Refine*	Emerge: *Transform*
	Attention: *Contact*	Affection: *Connect*	Appreciation: *Contribute*	Allow: *Cease*
Meanings & Mileposts	Precious: *Special*	Cherish: *Lovable*	Value: *Worth*	Honor: *Wisdom*
	Play: *Delight* "Happiness"	Passion: *Desire* "Satisfaction"	Purpose: *Determination* "Fulfillment"	Pause: *Deference/Devotion* "Peace"
Mastery & Mystery	Balance to integrity	Harmonize to intimacy	Synchronize to identity	Compose to integration
	Become ... Beauty	Belong ... Love	Believe ... Truth	Be ... Sacred

(Note: For those interested in the fundamental underpinnings of the organization of this book, you may read the Appendix to the Introduction to *Maps & Metaphors*. It discusses the *parssitern paradigm*, which proposes that all aspects of ourselves and the world are universally composed of *parts*, *processes*, *principles*, and a *pattern* that unites and integrates them. This is the *1, 2, 3* and the *3-in-1* that gives the book its title.)

THE THREE RELATIONSHIPS AND THE FOURTH THAT ENABLES THEM

Be Re-composed & Reborn
(as a child of God's Light & Love)

ENTER THE KINGDOM OF HEAVEN

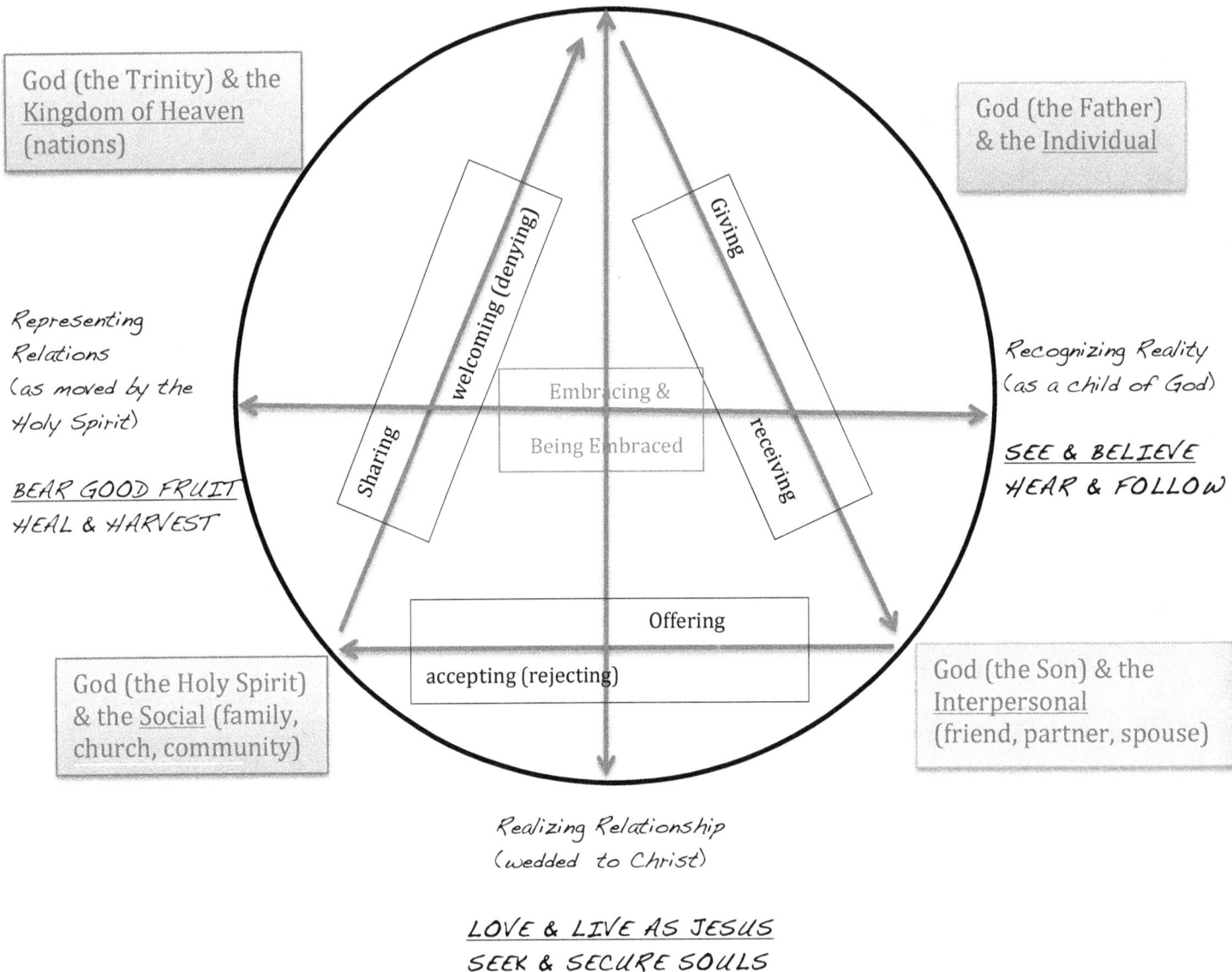

God (the Trinity) & the
<u>Kingdom of Heaven</u>
(nations)

God (the Father)
& the <u>Individual</u>

Representing
Relations
(as moved by the
Holy Spirit)

Recognizing Reality
(as a child of God)

welcoming (denying)

Giving

Sharing

Embracing &

Being Embraced

receiving

Offering

accepting (rejecting)

SEE & BELIEVE
HEAR & FOLLOW

<u>BEAR GOOD FRUIT</u>
HEAL & HARVEST

God (the Holy Spirit)
& the <u>Social</u> (family,
church, community)

God (the Son) & the
<u>Interpersonal</u>
(friend, partner, spouse)

Realizing Relationship
(wedded to Christ)

LOVE & LIVE AS JESUS
SEEK & SECURE SOULS

1. God *gives* and the person *receives*.

2. The person *offers* another person Christ and the other person *accepts* (or rejects).

3. Persons (disciples) who have received & accepted, seek to *share* the Word
   (Holy Spirit) with others & are *welcomed* (or denied).

4. *Embracing* Jesus Christ enables us to *be embraced* and move along this path.

A New Map of the Masterful Method of Jesus

Damian & Christina Vraniak

Organization of *Light Musings and Brief Illuminations*

I	II	III	[Mystery]
PARTS (within)	**PROCESSES** (between)	**PRINCIPLES** (among)	**PATTERN** (through)
Physical (continuous contact)	Recognizing Reality (as a child of God)	Preserving Beauty (Father: *Creator, Provider*)	Initiating, Instructing
Emotional (caring connection)	Realizing Relationship (wedded to Christ)	Restoring Love (Son: *Savior*)	Illuminating
Mental (considerate contribution)	Representing Relations (moved by the Holy Spirit)	Conserving Truth (Spirit: *Words, Works, Witness*)	Informing, Revealing
Spiritual (composition)	Recomposing (penetrated by the Holy Trinity)	Consecrating Sacred (Trinity: *Transformation*)	Inspiring, Sanctifying

You may instruct the body, illuminate the heart, inform the mind, and inspire the soul.

Jesus, and then Paul, prioritized these, saying that while the ***law*** may instruct the body (do's and don'ts) which informs the mind, this mind-body connection is always incomplete, fails and dies, meaning that the Tree of Knowledge (of Good and Evil) results in death; rather it is ***love*** that illuminates the heart and inspires the soul, more potently sustaining life continuously, in perpetuity, everlastingly, which is the other Tree in the garden, the Tree of Everlasting Life. Thus sayeth the Lord, love with all you heart and soul and mind (in that order), and thus sayeth Saul who became the Apostle Paul, that through the Spirit we eagerly await by faith the righteousness for which we hope, that the only thing that counts is faith expressing itself through love.

So, it is the heart-soul connection that is more and most important, over and above the mind-body connection! Those who would account continuously what we should and should not do according to the law are condemned, while those who faithfully embrace the Spirit-in-love are consecrated in Christ Jesus and moved by the Holy Spirit imagining, creating and inspiring abundant life.

Damian

Appendix E. *Dialectio Communitas Divina*

A New Map of the Masterful Method of Jesus

Damian & Christina Vraniak

Dialectio Communitas Divina

1. Individual Self-reflection: Read, meditate, pray, contemplate.   (*Instruct* ... (lectio Divina) recognize & preserve Beauty)

This reflection is emptying and opening in order to attend to God speaking through Scripture. See & believe. Hear & Follow.

2. Pair-Dialogue: Read, examine, make contrition/repent, pray.   (*Illuminate* ... reconcile & restore Love)

This refraction is an examination of my life in order to attach to God's presence and instruction. Feel remorse at failure. Repent.

3. Pair-sharing to group: Read, share, converse, pray.   (*Inform* ... reveal & conserve Truth)

This revelation is a seeking and sharing of forgiveness in community. Witness the Word into Works. Share salvation, save souls.

4. Blessing and Benediction: Convey transformation.   (*Inspire* ... sanctify & consecrate the Sacred)

This re-composing is finding the comfort and peace of atonement. Be re-born and begin anew.

1. INDIVIDUAL SELF-REFLECTION

Lectio ("read")

These are the things God has revealed to us by his Spirit. The Spirit searches all things, even the deep things of God
— 1 Corinthians 2:9–10. The first step is the reading of Scripture. In order to achieve a calm and tranquil state of mind, preparation before *Lectio Divina* is recommended. The biblical reference for preparation via stillness is Psalm 46:10: "Be still, and know that I am God." An example would be sitting quietly and in silence and reciting a prayer inviting the Holy Spirit to guide the reading of the Scripture that is to follow. The biblical basis for the preparation goes back to 1 Corinthians 2:9–10 which emphasizes the role of the Holy Spirit in revealing the Word of God. As in the statement by John the Baptist in John 1:26 that "Christ stands in the midst of those who seek him", the preparatory step should open the mind to finding Christ in the passage being read. Following the preparation the first movement of *Lectio Divina* is slow and gradual reading of the scriptural passage, perhaps several times. The biblical basis for the reading goes back to Romans 10:8–10 and the presence of God's word in the believer's "mouth or heart". The attentive reading begins the process through which a higher level of understanding can be achieved. In the traditional Benedictine approach the passage is slowly read four times, each time with a slightly different focus.

Meditatio ("meditate")

Although *Lectio Divina* involves reading, it is less a practice of reading than one of listening to the inner message of the Scripture delivered through the Holy Spirit. *Lectio Divina* does not seek information or motivation, but communion with God. It does not treat Scripture as text to be studied, but as the "Living Word". The second movement in *Lectio Divina* thus involves meditating upon and pondering on the scriptural passage. When the passage is read, it is generally advised not to try to assign a meaning to it at first, but to wait for the action of the Holy Spirit to illuminate the mind, as the passage is pondered upon. The English word ponder comes from the Latin *pondus* which relates to the mental activity of weighing or considering. To ponder on the passage that has been read, it is held lightly and gently considered from various angles. Again, the emphasis is not on analysis of the passage but to keep the mind open and allow the Holy Spirit to inspire a meaning for it. An example passage may be the statement by Jesus during the Last Supper in John 14:27: "Peace I leave with you; my peace I give unto you". An analytical approach would focus on why Jesus said that, the fact that it was said at the Last Supper, and the context within the biblical episode. Other theological analysis may follow, e.g. the cost at which Jesus the Lamb of God provided peace through his obedience to the will of Father, etc. However, these theological analyses are generally avoided in *Lectio Divina*, where the focus is on Christ as the key that interprets the passage and relates it to the meditator. So rather than "dissecting peace" in an analytical manner, the practitioner of *Lectio Divina* "enters peace" and shares the peace of Christ. The focus will thus be on achieving peace via a closer communion with God rather than a biblical analysis of the passage. Similar other passages may be "Abide in my love", "I am the Good Shepherd", etc.

Oratio ("pray")

In the Christian tradition, prayer is understood as dialogue with God, that is, as loving conversation with God who has invited us into an embrace. The constitution *Dei verbum* which endorsed *Lectio Divina* for the general public, as well as in monastic settings, quoted Saint Ambrose on the importance of prayer in conjunction with Scripture reading and stated: And let them remember that prayer should accompany the reading of Sacred Scripture, so that God and man may talk together; for "we speak to Him when we pray; we hear Him when we read the divine saying. Pope Benedict XVI emphasized the importance of using *Lectio Divina* and prayers on Scripture as a guiding light and a source of direction and stated: It should never be forgotten that the Word of God is a lamp for our feet and a light for our path.

Contemplatio ("contemplate")

Contemplation takes place in terms of silent prayer that expresses love for God. The Catechism of the Catholic Church defines contemplative prayer as "the hearing the Word of God" in an attentive mode. It states: Contemplative prayer is silence, the "symbol of the world to come" or "silent love." Words in this kind of prayer are not speeches; they are like kindling that feeds the fire of love. In this silence, unbearable to the "outer" man, the Father speaks to us his incarnate Word, who suffered, died, and rose; in this silence the Spirit of adoption enables us to share in the prayer of Jesus. The role of the Holy Spirit in contemplative prayer has been emphasized by Christian spiritual writers for centuries. In the 12th century, Saint Bernard of Clairvaux compared the Holy Spirit to a kiss by the Eternal Father which allows the practitioner of contemplative prayer to experience union with God. In the 14th century, Richard Rolle viewed contemplation as the path that leads the soul to union with God in love, and considered the Holy Spirit as the center of contemplation. From a theological perspective, God's grace is considered a principle, or cause, of contemplation, with its benefits delivered through the gifts of the Holy Spirit.

The progression from Bible reading, to meditation, to prayer, to loving regard for God, was first formally described by Guigo II, a Carthusian monk and prior of Grande Chartreuse who died late in the 12th century. The Carthusian order follows its own Rule, called the Statutes, rather than the Rule of St Benedict. Guigo II's book *The Ladder of Monks* is subtitled "a letter on the contemplative life" and is considered the first description of methodical prayer in the western mystical tradition. In Guigo's four stages one first reads, which leads to think about (i.e. meditate on) the significance of the text; that process in turn leads the person to respond in prayer as the third stage. The fourth stage is when the prayer, in turn, points to the gift of quiet stillness in the presence of God, called contemplation. Guigo named the four steps of this "ladder" of prayer with the Latin terms *lectio*, *meditatio*, *oratio*, and *contemplatio*.

In 1965, one of the principal documents of the Second Vatican Council, the dogmatic constitution *Dei verbum* ("Word of God") emphasized the use of *Lectio Divina*. On the 40th anniversary of *Dei verbum* in 2005, Pope Benedict XVI reaffirmed its importance and stated: I would like in particular to recall and recommend the ancient tradition of *Lectio Divina*: the diligent reading of Sacred Scripture accompanied by prayer brings about that intimate dialogue in which the person reading hears God who is speaking, and in praying, responds to him with trusting openness of heart. In his November 6, 2005 Angelus address, Benedict XVI emphasized the role of the Holy Spirit in *Lectio Divina*: In his annual Lenten addresses to the priests of the Diocese of Rome, Pope Benedict – mainly after the 2008 Synod of Bishops on the Bible – emphasized *Lectio Divina*' s importance, as in 2012, when he used Ephesians 4: 1–16 on a speech about certain problems facing the Church. Beforehand, he and Pope John Paul II had used a question-and-answer format. One condition for *Lectio Divina* is that the mind and heart be illumined by the Holy Spirit, that is, by the same Spirit who inspired the Scriptures, and that they be approached with an attitude of "reverential hearing".

2. PAIR-DIALOGUE REFRACTION

Spiritual direction is the practice of being with people as they attempt to deepen their relationship with the divine, or to learn and grow in their own personal spirituality. The person seeking direction shares stories of his or her encounters of the divine, or how he or she is experiencing spiritual issues. The director listens and asks questions to assist the directee in his or her process of reflection and spiritual growth. Spiritual direction develops a deeper relationship with the spiritual aspect of being human. It is not psychotherapy, counseling, or financial planning. While there is some degree of variability, there are primarily two forms of spiritual direction: regular direction and retreat direction. They differ largely in the frequency of meeting and in the intensity of reflection. Regular direction can involve a one to two hour meeting every four to eight weeks, and thus is slightly less intense than retreat direction, although spiritual exercises and disciplines are often given for the directee to attempt between meetings.

If the directee is on a retreat (lasting a weekend, a week or even 40 days), he or she will generally meet with his or her director on a daily basis for one hour. During these daily meetings, exercises or spiritual disciplines such as lectio divina are given to the directee as fodder to continue his or her spiritual growth. Alternatively, retreat centres often offer direction or companionship to persons visiting the centre alone. The Spiritual Exercises of Ignatius of Loyola are a popular example of guidelines used for spiritual direction.

Historical Traditions

Western Christianity

Within Christianity, spiritual direction has its roots in the Early Christianity. The gospels describe Jesus serving as a mentor to his disciples. Additionally, Acts of the Apostles Chapter 9 describes Ananias helping Paul of Tarsus to grow in his newfound experience of Christianity. Likewise, several of the Pauline epistles describe Paul mentoring both Timothy and Titus among others. Tradition tells that

John the Evangelist tutored Polycarp, the 2nd-century bishop of Smyrna. John Cassian who lived in the 4th century provided some of the earliest recorded guidelines on the Christian practice of spiritual direction. He introduced mentoring in the monasteries. Each novice was put under the care of an older monk. Benedict of Nursia integrated Cassian's guidelines into what is now known as the Rule of Saint Benedict.

Eastern Orthodoxy

Eastern Orthodoxy comes from the same pre-schism traditions, but the role of a "spiritual director" or "elder" in Orthodoxy has maintained its important role. The original Greek term geron (meaning "elder", as in gerontology) was rendered by the Russian word starets, from Old Church Slavonic starĭtsĭ, "elder", derived from starŭ, "old". The Greek tradition has a long unbroken history of elders and disciples, such as Sophronius and John Moschos in the seventh century, Symeon the Elder and Symeon the New Theologian in the eleventh century, and contemporary charismatic gerontes such as Porphyrios and Paisios. Sergius of Radonezh and Nil Sorsky were two most venerated startsy of Old Muscovy. The revival of elders in the Slavic world is associated with the name of Paisius Velichkovsky (1722–94), who produced the Russian translation of the Philokalia. The most famous Russian starets of the early 19th century was Seraphim of Sarov (1759-1833), who went on to become one of the most revered Orthodox saints. The Optina Pustyn near Kozelsk used to be celebrated for its startsy (Schema-Archimandrite Moses, Schema-Hegumen Anthony, Hieroschemamonk Leonid, Hieroschemamonk Macarius, Hieroschemamonk Hilarion, Hieroschemamonk Ambrose, Hieroschemamonk Anatole (Zertsalov)). Such writers as Nikolay Gogol, Aleksey Khomyakov, Leo Tolstoy and Konstantin Leontyev sought advice from the elders of this monastery. They also inspired the figure of Zosima in Dostoyevsky's novel The Brothers Karamazov. A more modern example of a starets is Archimandrite John Krestiankin (1910-2006) of the Pskov Monastery of the Caves who was popularly recognized as such by many Orthodox living in Russia.

Judaism

In Judaism, the Hebrew term for spiritual director differs among traditional communities. The verb *Hashpa'ah* is common in some communities though not all; the spiritual director called a *mashpi'a* occurs in the Habad-Lubavitch community and also in the Jewish Renewal community. A *mashgiakh ruchani* is the equivalent role among mitnagedim (adherents of the *mussar* tradition). The purpose of hashpa'ah is to support the directee in her or his personal relationship with God, and to deepen that person's ability to find God's presence in ordinary life. Amongst Lubavitchers this draws on the literature and praxis of Hasidism as it is practiced according to Habad standards, and to Jewish mystical tradition generally. Spiritual mentorship is customary in the Hasidic world, but not necessarily in the same way.

Sufism

In Sufism, the term used for spiritual master is *murshid*, Arabic for "guide" or "teacher". He is more than a spiritual director and believed to be guiding the disciples based on his direct connectivity with the Divine. The murshid's role is to spiritually guide and verbally instruct the disciple on the Sufi path after the disciple takes an oath of allegiance or Bay'ah (*bai'ath*) with him. The concept of Murshid Kamil Akmal (also known as Insan-e-Kamil) is significant in most tariqas. The doctrine states that from pre-existence till pre-eternity, there shall always remain a Qutb or a Universal Man upon the earth who would be the perfect manifestation of God and at the footsteps of the Islamic prophet Mohammad.

What is Spiritual Accompaniment (Direction)?

Spiritual Accompaniment, traditionally known as Spiritual Direction, is a process through which one might become more deeply attuned to one's relationship with the Divine. Through conversation with a spiritual companion in an atmosphere of trust, a person comes to a deeper awareness of the presence and movement of God in their everyday life. As those accompanied share their dreams, struggles, triumphs and fears, they open to their deepest and wisest source of freedom and joy. A spiritual companion helps a person notice, savour and respond to the movement of the Divine in the spiritual practice of ordinary life. The companion is a listening and supportive person who creates an environment where one can look honestly at his or her relationship with the Sacred.

The operative word in our definition is "relationship". Spiritual accompaniment is always aimed ultimately at fostering union with God and has therefore to do with the individual's relationship with God. The spiritual journey is about the movement towards unity of self in God, the movement towards wholeness (holiness).

The Rite of the Sacrament of Reconciliation

Reconciliation may be face-to-face or anonymous, with a screen between you and the priest.

1 The priest gives you a blessing or greeting. He may share a brief Scripture passage.
2 Make the Sign of the Cross and say: ***"Bless me father, for I have sinned. My last confession was..."*** (number of wks/mos/yrs).
3 Confess all of your sins to the priest. The priest will help you to make a good confession. If you are unsure about how to confess or you feel uneasy, just ask him to help you. Answer his questions without hiding anything out of fear or shame. Place your trust in God, a merciful Father who wants to forgive you.
4 Following your confession of sins, say: ***"I am sorry for these and all of my sins."***
5 The priest assigns you a penance and offers advice to help you be a better Catholic.
6 Say an Act of Contrition, expressing your sorrow for your sins. The priest, acting in the person of Christ, then absolves you from your sins.

Act of Contrition
God, I am heartily sorry for having offended you, and I detest all my sins because I dread the loss of heaven and the pains of hell; but most of all because they offend you, my God, who are all good and deserving of all my love. I firmly resolve with the help of your grace to confess my sins, do penance, and to amend my life. Amen.

The **Sacrament of Penance & Reconciliation** (commonly called **Confession**, **Reconciliation** or **Penance**) is one of seven sacraments of the Catholic Church and sacred mysteries of Eastern Christianity, in which the faithful obtain divine mercy for the sins committed against God and neighbour and are reconciled with the community of the Church. By this sacrament Christians are freed from sins committed after Baptism. The sacrament of Penance is considered the normal way to be absolved from mortal sins which would otherwise condemn a person to Hell.[3] As biblical basis for this sacrament, the Catholic Church refers to James 5:16, "confess your sins to one another" and to Jesus' breathing the Holy Spirit to the Apostles, saying "Whose sins you forgive are forgiven them, and whose sins you retain are retained" (John 20:23).Beginnings of practising the sacrament of penance in the form of individual confession as we know it now, i.e. bringing confession of sins and reconciliation together, can be traced back to 11th century. In 1215 the Fourth Council of the Lateran made it canon law that every Catholic Christian goes to confession in his parish at least once a year. The specification to one's own parish was later dropped.

Although the issue of the institution of this sacrament by Jesus himself had been debated since the Council of Trent, in 1907 in *Lamentabili sane exitu* Pope Pius X specifically reaffirmed the relevance of Gospel of John 20:22-23 to this sacrament, overriding any previous assertions. In *Lamentabili sane exitu* he quoted John 20:22-23: "Receive the Holy Spirit. Whose sins you forgive are forgiven them, and whose sins you retain are retained."In the early Church, publicly known sins were often confessed openly or publicly in church.[25] However, private confession was still used for private sins.[25] Also, penance was often done before absolution rather than after absolution.[25] Penances, also known as satisfaction, are assigned to expiate what is called the temporal punishment that remains due to sins even when the sins are forgiven, namely "an unhealthy attachment to creatures, which must be purified either here on earth, or after death in the state called Purgatory".[26] In the early Church, the assigned penances were much more harsh. For example, it would not have been unusual for someone to receive a 10-year penance[25] for committing the sin of abortion which the Catholic Church considers to be a grave or mortal sin.[27] With more of an emphasis later placed on the Church's ability to expiate temporal effects of sin (by prayer, sacramentals and indulgences and most especially by The Sacrifice of the Mass) penances began to be lessened or mitigated.

The current rite of the sacrament of Reconciliation was given to the Church by Pope Paul VI on December 2, 1973. The 1973 rite presents the sacrament in three different ritual forms:

The Rite for Reconciliation of Individual Penitents — is similar to the way most Roman Catholics remember "confession"; however, provision is made for the reading of sacred Scripture, and the penitent is given the option of speaking to the priest face-to-face or remaining anonymous (usually behind a screen). The priest gives a suitable penance and may offer advice. The priest pronounces absolution (the formula of absolution was revised and extended) and the rite concludes with a short thanksgiving.[41]

The Rite of Reconciliation of Several Penitents with Individual Confession and Absolution — usually begins with readings from scripture, hymns, prayers, a homily and an examination of conscience, followed by a call to repentance. Private confession and reconciliation follow and a final thanksgiving, blessing and dismissal. Paul VI said in 1974 that he hoped this communal rite would "become the normal way of celebration."

The Rite for Reconciliation of Several Penitents with General Confession and Absolution — is similar to the second, except that the penitents do not make an actual confession, but only manifest contrition (general confession). The prayer of absolution is given collectively or "generally" to all those gathered to celebrate the sacrament (general absolution). The penitents are obliged to actually confess each grave sin in their next confession.[42] This form is intended for emergencies and other situations when it is not at all possible for the priest(s) to hear all the individual confessions. This rite has been discouraged for widespread use by the Vatican in many countries recently.

3. PAIR-SHARING TO GROUP

Torah reading (Hebrew: התורה קריאת, *K'riat HaTorah* ; "Reading [of] the Torah"; Yiddish: *Kriyas HaToire*) is a Jewish religious tradition that involves the public reading of a set of passages from a Torah scroll. The term often refers to the entire ceremony of removing the Torah scroll (or scrolls) from the ark, chanting the appropriate excerpt with special cantillation, and returning the scroll(s) to the ark. Regular public reading of the Torah was introduced by Ezra the Scribe after the return of the Judean exiles from the Babylonian captivity (c. 537 BCE), as described in the Book of Nehemiah.[1] In the modern era, adherents of Orthodox Judaism practice Torah reading according to a set procedure they believe has remained unchanged in the two thousand years since the destruction of the Temple in Jerusalem (70 CE). In the 19th and 20th centuries CE, Reform Judaism and Conservative Judaism have made adaptations to the practice of Torah reading, but the basic pattern of Torah reading has usually remained the same:

As a part of the morning or afternoon prayer services on certain days of the week or holidays, a section of the Pentateuch is read from a Torah scroll. On Shabbat (Saturday) mornings, a weekly section (known as a *Sedra* or *parashah*) is read, selected so that the entire Pentateuch is read consecutively each year.[2][3][4][5] On

129

Saturday afternoons, Mondays, and Thursdays, the beginning of the following Saturday's portion is read. On Jewish holidays, Rosh Chodesh, and fast days, special sections connected to the day are read. Religious Jews observe an annual holiday, Simchat Torah, to celebrate the completion of the year's cycle of readings.

Lection

A Scripture lesson being read in a service of Nine Lessons and Carols.
A **lection**, also called the **lesson**, is a reading from Scripture in Liturgy.

The custom of reading the books of Moses in the synagogues on Sabbath is a very ancient one. Since the prophetic books were written after the books of Moses, readings from them began later, but were in existence at the time of Jesus. This element in synagogue worship was taken over with others into the Christian divine service, as may be gathered from passages in the gospels such as St Luke 4:16–20 and 16:29. During early Christianity, readings began to be made from the writings of the Apostles and evangelists as the New Testament canon developed. Mention of this is found within the New Testament itself, for example in Colossians 4:16 and in First Thessalonians 5:27. The oldest manuscripts of the Gospels have marginal marks, and sometimes actual interpolations, which can only be accounted for as indicating the beginnings and endings of liturgical lessons.
From the 2nd century onwards references multiply, though the earlier references do not prove the existence of a fixed lectionary or order of lessons, but rather point the other way. Justin Martyr, describing divine worship in the middle of the 2nd century says: "On the day called Sunday all who live in cities or in the country gather together to one place, and the memoirs of the Apostles, or the writings of the Prophets are read as long as time permits" (*Apol.* i. cap. 67). Tertullian about half a century later makes frequent reference to the reading of Holy Scripture in public worship (*Apol.* ~9; *De praescript.* 36; *De amina*, 9).

The canons of Hippolytus, written in the first half of the 3rd century says, "Let presbyters, subdeacons and readers, and all the people assemble daily in the church at time of cockcrow, and betake themselves to prayers, to psalms and to the reading of the Scriptures, according to the command of the Apostles, until I come attend to reading" (canon xxi). There are traces of fixed lessons coming into existence in the course of the 3rd century. Origen refers to the Book of Job being read in Holy Week (*Commentaries on Job*, lib. i.). In the 4th century are such references are frequent. John Cassian (c. 380) states that throughout Egypt the Psalms were divided into groups of twelve, and that after each group there followed two lessons, one from the Old Testament and one from the New Testament (*De caenob. inst.* ii. 4), implying but not absolutely stating that there was a fixed order of such lessons just as there was of the Psalms. St Basil the Great mentions fixed lessons on certain occasions taken from Isaiah, Proverbs, St Matthew and Acts (Hom. xiii. *De bapt.*). From Chrysostom (Horn. lxiii. in Act. etc.), and Augustine (Tract. vi. in Joann. &c.) both state that Genesis was read in Lent, Job and Jonah in Passion Week, the Acts of the Apostles in Eastertide, lessons on the Passion on Good Friday, and lessons on the Resurrection on Easter Day.

In the Apostolical Constitutions (ii. 57, ca. 380) a service is described which is required of the church. First come two lessons from the Old Testament by a reader, the whole of the Old Testament being made use of except the books of the Apocrypha. The Psalms of David are then to be sung. Next the Acts of the Apostles and the Epistles of Paul are to be read. Finally the four Gospels are to be read by a deacon or a priest. Whether the selections were ad libitum or according to a fixed table of lessons is not mentioned.

The third Council of Carthage in 397 forbade anything but Holy Scripture to be read in church. This rule has been adhered to so far as the liturgical epistle and gospel, and occasional additional lessons in the Roman missal are concerned, but in the divine office, on feasts when nine lessons are read at matins, only the first three lessons are taken from Holy Scripture, the next three being taken from the sermons of ecclesiastical writers, and the last three from expositions of the day's gospel; but sometimes the lives or Passions of the saints, or of some particular saints, were substituted for any or all of these breviary lessons.

Nothing in the shape of a lectionary is extant older than the 8th century, though there is evidence that Claudianus Marnercus made one for the church at Vienna in 450, and that Musaeus made one for the church at Marseilles ca. 458.

Intensive group meditation

Intensive group meditation may be practiced occasionally in some temples. In the Japanese language, this practice is called *Sesshin*. While the daily routine may require monks to meditate for several hours each day, during the intensive period they devote themselves almost exclusively to the practice of sitting meditation. The numerous 30–50 minute long meditation periods are interwoven with rest breaks, meals, and short periods of work that are performed with the same mindfulness; nightly sleep is kept to seven hours or less. In modern Buddhist practice in Japan, Taiwan, and the West, lay students often attend these intensive practice sessions, which are typically 1, 3, 5, or 7 days in length. These are held at many Zen centers, especially in commemoration of the Buddha's attainment of *Anuttarā Samyaksaṃbodhi*. One distinctive aspect of Zen meditation in groups is the use of a kyosaku, a flat, wooden slat used to strike meditators with the intention of keeping them focused and awake.

Insight - Kōan practice[edit]

Chinese character for "nothing", Chinese: wú (Japanese: mu). It figures in the famous *Zhaozhou's dog* kōan

At the beginning of the Song Dynasty, practice with the kōan method became popular, whereas others practiced "silent illumination."[12] This became the source of some differences in practice between the Linji and Caodong traditions.
A kōan, literally "public case", is a story or dialogue, describing an interaction between a Zen master and a student. These anecdotes give a demonstration of the

master's insight. Koans emphasize the non-conceptional insight that the Buddhist teachings are pointing to. Koans can be used to provoke the "great doubt", and test a student's progress in Zen practice.

Kōan-inquiry may be practiced during sitting meditation (*zazen*), walking meditation (*kinhin*), and throughout all the activities of daily life. Kōan practice is particularly emphasized by the Japanese Rinzai school, but it also occurs in other schools or branches of Zen depending on the teaching line.[13] The Zen student's mastery of a given kōan is presented to the teacher in a private interview (referred to in Japanese as dokusan (独参), daisan (代参), or sanzen (参禅)). While there is no unique answer to a kōan, practitioners are expected to demonstrate their understanding of the kōan and of Zen through their responses. The teacher may approve or disapprove of the answer and guide the student in the right direction. The interaction with a Zen-teacher is central in Zen, but makes Zen-practice, at least in the west, also vulnerable to misunderstanding and exploitation.[14]

Sounds[edit]
The Orthodox Church traditionally does not use any instruments in the liturgy, instead relying entirely on choral music and chanting. Essentially all the words of Orthodox services, except sermons and such, are either chanted or sung by readers and choirs and when possible the congregations.

Chanting
Nothing in Orthodox worship is simply said; it is always sung or chanted. Chanting in the Orthodox tradition can be described as being halfway between talking and singing; it is musical but not music. One or two notes only are used in chanting, and the chanter reads the words to these notes at a steady rhythm. The notes and rhythms used vary according to what the occasion is, but generally chanting is relatively low-toned and steadily rhythmic creating a calming sound. Chanting not only is conducive to a calm and elevated state of mind but also allows chanters to read through large portions of texts (particularly Psalms) more clearly and quickly than possible with normal speech while also conveying the poetry in the words. That is the essential reason for chanting. Worship at its heart is a song and is beautiful; therefore the words of Orthodox worship cannot be simply said but must be melodiously chanted to express the true nature and purpose of the words.

Singing
Words not chanted in Orthodox worship are sung by a choir. Originally singing was done by the entire congregation, however this rapidly became cumbersome and a select group of singers was selected to represent the congregation. Since then Orthodox church music has expanded and become more elaborate. The Church uses eight 'tones' or 'modes,' which are broad categories of melodies. Within each of these tones are many small more precise melodies. All of these tones and their melodies rotate weekly so that during each week a particular tone is used for singing music. Singing naturally developed from chanting but, unlike in the west, Orthodox music developed from a Greek musical background. Even though

Orthodoxy has spread and its music adapted to its various regions, still Orthodox music is distinctive from European music. Singing is used in place of chanting on important occasions thus some things which are chanted at minor services are sung at more important services. Singing is as varied and multi-faceted in its forms as chanting and vestments, it changes with the Church 'seasons' of commemoration thus singing during Great Lent is always somber and during Holy Week nearly becomes a sorrowful dirge while during Pascha (Easter) and the Paschal season the notes are high and quick and as joyful as they were sad during Lent. The power of music is not lost on the Orthodox and it is used to its full effect to bring about spiritual renewal in the listeners.

Chant as a spiritual practice

Chanting (e.g., mantra, sacred text, the name of God/Spirit, etc.) is a commonly used spiritual practice. Like prayer, chant may be a component of either personal or group practice. Diverse spiritual traditions consider chant a route to spiritual development.

Monks chanting, Drepung monastery, Tibet, 2013

Some examples include chant in African, Hawaiian, and Native American, and Australian Aboriginal cultures, Gregorian chant, Vedic chant, Qur'an reading, Islamic Dhikr, Baha'i chants, various Buddhist chants, various mantras, Jewish cantillation, and the chanting of psalms and prayers especially in Roman Catholic (see Gregorian chant or Taizé Community), Eastern Orthodox (see Byzantine chant or Znamenny chant, for examples), Lutheran, and Anglican churches (see Anglican Chant).

Chant practices vary. Tibetan Buddhist chant involves throat singing, where multiple pitches are produced by each performer. The concept of chanting mantras is of particular significance in many Hindu traditions and other closely related Dharmic Religions. India's bhakti devotional tradition centres on kirtan, which has a following in many countries and traditions such as Ananda Marga. The Hare Krishna movement is based especially on the chanting of Sanskrit Names of God in the Vaishnava tradition. Japanese *Shigin* (詩吟), or 'chanted poetry', mirrors Zen Buddhist principles and is sung from the *Dan tien* (or lower abdomen) — the locus of power in Eastern traditions.

www.ingramcontent.com/pod-product-compliance
Lightning Source LLC
Chambersburg PA
CBHW081255040426

42452CB00014B/2509